Selected Works of Julio Meinvielle

Volume 3

The Catholic Understanding of the Economy

THE CATHOLIC UNDERSTANDING OF THE ECONOMY

JULIO MEINVIELLE

Translated by Nathaniel Dreyer

IVE PRESS

Title of Spanish original
Concepción católica de la economía

ISBN (paperback): 978-1-947568-64-8
ISBN (ebook): 978-1-947568-65-5

Library of Congress Control Number: 2025937938

Printed in the United States of America

Table of Contents

ABOUT THE TRANSLATOR

Originally from Ypsilanti, Michigan, Nathaniel Dreyer, a member of the Institute of the Incarnate Word religious order, completed his undergraduate studies at the University of Michigan in Ann Arbor, earning a degree in Spanish, Czech, and general biology. He was ordained a priest in 2015 after having completed a licentiate in philosophy at The Catholic University of America, and is currently a doctoral candidate in philosophy at the Pontifical Athenaeum Regina Apostolorum in Rome.

TRANSLATOR'S PREFACE

What follows is a translation of Julio Meinvielle's book, *Concepción católica de la economía* (Buenos Aires: Cursos de cultura católica, 1936). For more information about Julio Meinvielle and his works, see www.juliomeinvielle.org.

Unless otherwise noted, all translations of St. Thomas Aquinas' work into English are taken from the Aquinas Institute edition available at www.aquinas.cc.

This text uses two sets of footnotes. The first set, designated with Arabic numerals, are the author's original notes; the only changes introduced in this set were to standardize names and references and to replace texts quoted in a language other than Spanish with an English translation. Occasionally a reference has been changed to "cf." when the text does not match the Latin original. The second set, indicated with letters, includes the texts as quoted by the author in their original language, the citations for the translations utilized, and comments regarding the author's original text.

Author's Prologue

"But seek first the kingdom [of God] and his righteousness and all these things will be given you besides," [Mt 6:33] said Jesus Christ.

These words are not a pious maxim. They are a law of reality. The modern world, which wants to seek economic goods above all else, not only does not obtain those goods, but has also lost the kingdom of God.

This book aims to set the record straight. Above all, it wishes to show that the Gospel and the Church's doctrine—expressed so wonderfully by Saint Thomas Aquinas—contain the essential principles of human life, which no economy can forget.

The economy does not have an end in itself, as if it were a god. The economy is based on man. It must serve man, and not a man forged in the philosopher's mind, but at the service of real man, as a creature created by God with all the hierarchical potencies that it contains.

If this commonsense truth is forgotten, then one runs the risk of forging truly wonderful but disastrous creations.

This is what happens with modern economic systems and with the theories of economists, which seem to be extremely grandiose constructions. But what are they worth if instead of serving, they sacrifice the human community?

It is sad to contemplate the waste of the complicated skills of many economists in admirable fantasies that fall into emptiness because they do not bear in mind this elementary truth: that economics is valuable to the extent that it benefits man. For this reason, this book is not and cannot be a technical book. It is simply a common-sense reflection on the realities of economic life.

When economic life is ordered with a human emphasis, skills can play a beneficial role, making the various organs of economic activity more in accord with human efficiency.

But if this human ordering is lacking, any skill will be fruitless, if not evil.

It is not that skills are to be despised. Skills have a useful but secondary mission. Skills are inherently myopic. They must be illuminated by the higher senses. It is possible, e.g., for example, that, in the "set x of economic phenomena," one who possesses the requisite skills can compare the financial movements and discover a progress in the activities that can be translated into an ascension of mathematical curves; but does it follow that real economic life has progressed, bringing real improvements in wealth and well-being to all who have acted in "set x of economic phenomena"? Is it not possible that this progress of curves indicates a real increase in the total set, but since there is inequality in the distribution, this progress has been made for the benefit of a few and at the expense of the social body? And where skills have been made to verify a progress of curves, the truth of human well-being indicates a decline? Isn't it clear that there has never been in the history of humanity a financial movement, especially stock market, as enormous as today, and yet, when compared to other times, human well-being is no better?

This shows that the shortsightedness of skills must be illuminated by higher views of the intelligence. Of the intelligence, I say, that sees the reason and essence of things. This intelligence is called *common sense* when it proceeds well by its own instinct to reach the truth, and is called

Aristotelean-Thomistic philosophy when it can reflexively justify that it is advancing rightly.

Hence this book is, in truth, a Catholic philosophy of economics. But by saying philosophy, let no one think that it is a capricious creation of the mind. The true philosophy is nothing more than the reflective penetration into beings, trying to determine their essential laws. The authentic philosopher neither creates nor invents, but reads.

For this reason, this book intends to highlight the essential organization of any economy that is truly at the service of man: simply, of the economy. This is because an economy that does not serve man is a contradiction. It would be an anti-economic economy.

It must serve the whole man with the hierarchical potentialities that he contains. Man is not simply a stomach. In addition to his stomach, man is also rational; in addition to being a man, he has, by God's mercy, a divine destiny. The economy must provide the social man with the goods for his body, so that man might reach that divine destiny.

Only by respecting this essential law of man will the procurement of material goods truly be an economy.

Chapter 1

The Economy and the Modern Economy

THE WORLD LIVES TODAY under the sign of economic anxiety, because the meaning of the economy has been lost. An infinity of economic phenomena is known, called production, land, capital, work, finance, and consumption; so-called economic laws are noted; theories are built and economic schools are created; but the meaning of economy has not been grasped, because the meaning of human life has been lost.

The modern world—I call the modern world the one engendered by the anti-traditional action of the Protestant Reformation, perpetuated in nineteenth-century liberalism, and now ready to bury itself in Bolshevist anarchy—the modern world, I say, does not know and cannot know what life is, because it has been deprived of the proper act of intelligence, which is "to judge." In "judgment," the intelligence knows the real (ontological) value of things. It is an essentially teleological act. When faced with a being, the human person does not want to know so much its functioning, its mechanism, its phenomenal reality, as its essence determined by its end: "What is such a being for?" Once its purpose is known, its functioning can be made to match it.

For this reason, our constant concern in this book will be to formulate a value judgment on economic reality. We will have to penetrate into the very depths of modern economic phenomena, in order to discover their essential conformation and see if there is an innate perversion in them, and, if this is the case, to propose the conditions of an effective medicine. As the economic phenomena that surround us are essentially capitalist, nothing is fairer than specifying the nature of the capitalist economy.

MATTER AND FORM OF THE ECONOMY

In all concrete economic constructions, for example, the liberal capitalist economy, we can distinguish two different elements, substantially united in a single being; Using Aristotelian-Thomistic language, we will call matter the passive and formless element that receives as a soul and conformation the other element, which we will call form. From the substantial union of this matter with this form a concrete economic construction is produced, in the same way that every material being, water for example, results from a certain quantity of matter informed by the determining and specific principle, which is the form. Matter is a common element that can be informed by different forms, thus giving rise to different beings or essences. For example, when we drink water, and it becomes our flesh, the form of water disappears and gives way to that of flesh; however, the matter remains the same, and now supports the form of flesh as it once supported that of water. This means that there can successively be two different beings that have the same matter.

Let us apply this doctrine to the liberal capitalist economy. In it, the means of production, credit, the global exchange of products, for example, is like the material of the economic structure, and the configuration given to these elements is like the form. If these elements were given a different configuration, if they were determined by another form, a different economy could also emerge. For this reason, what is of interest for the knowledge of an economic structure is the determination of that formal principle that constitutes its soul.

However, the material elements are also of interest, since a particular form cannot inform matter if it is not found with certain favorable dispositions: thus, for example, the food we eat is not assimilated into our substance until after a process of transformation, carried out by the action of the gastro-intestinal juices, which dispose the matter for the reception of a certain form. For its part, the form, as it is substantially united to the matter, imprints a characteristic stamp on it.

This Aristotelian-Thomistic distinction of matter and form, applied to economics, is fundamental in order to specify the scope of the criticisms that will be formulated against capitalism. These criticisms will not touch upon the material elements (for example, the means of production, the world commercial exchange, capital), but rather the configuration that capitalism has imprinted on these material elements, the use it has made of the means of production, of capital.

Let us therefore specify the essence of the capitalist economy by determining its matter and form.

FORMAL ELEMENTS OF CAPITALISM

The form will be made clear to us by the state of man at the moment in which he indicates, in an official way, the impulse to the liberal capitalist economy. This happened towards the end of the 18th century, when, with the ancient world in its dying agony, physical-mathematical science with its technological applications, liberal democracy with the crushing of the aristocracy and exaltation of the bourgeois, and the political economy with the theories of the physiocrats[a] and the liberal school set out on a victorious race. At the same time, there were such outstanding events as American Independence, the French Revolution, the construction of the steam engine, and the freedom of trade.

What was the state of man at that very moment?

Man was on a downward slope, down which he had been rolling for more than three centuries. The Middle Ages had achieved a unique miracle in the history of human equilibrium. His passions calmed, man lived in peace with himself, and lived in peace with his brothers, in the hierarchical order of social life. There was order without violence, because all parts of society moved freely in the sphere of their functions, each in its own sphere, without absorbing the lower or trampling the higher. At the top of this hierarchically ordered social universe was the Servant of the servants of God, just as at the summit of human concerns was "the only thing necessary": the love of Him who manifested Himself to us as Father.

It is not about making the apology of medieval civilization, "more splendid still, no doubt, in the refined memories of history than in the reality of experience,"[1,b] but to glimpse the normal type of a human civilization.

Luther officially breaks this beautiful system by annihilating religious life, which, without aiming to, also supported man's intellectual and moral life. Without supernatural grace, the instincts of the human beast stood out,

---

1 Jacques Maritain, *Religion et culture* (Paris: Desclée, 1930).

---

a A member of an 18th-century group of French economists who believed that agriculture was the source of all wealth and that agricultural products should be highly priced. Advocating adherence to a supposed natural order of social institutions, they also stressed the necessity of free trade.

b Trans. from Jacques Maritain, "Religion and Culture," in *Essays in Order* (New York: Macmillan, 1931), 23.

especially greed, the execrable desire for riches, which is like idolatry, according to the Apostle.

"While the mercantilism of the sixteenth and seventeenth centuries heralds the liberalism of the nineteenth and Elizabeth's legalized piracy leaves modern speculators behind,"[2] Descartes and Kant, destroying the life of intelligence and substituting it with reason, that is: a faculty that does not perceive essences but only abstract, mechanical realities, of a comparable magnitude, lay the foundations of a physical economy, adjusted to invariable mechanical laws, like the course of the stars, and like it, removed from human oversight and governance.

The curious thing is that while the domination of greed and the rationalistic or mechanical understanding of life grew, it felt weakened inside and therefore anxious to break the rules that forced her to keep herself in order. Rousseau officially proclaims the era of all-encompassing freedom, because, since there is no God, there is no sovereign, and the individual man himself establishes his own law.

On the other hand, Rousseau coincides with the exhaustion of the Protestant and rationalist impulse, and, therefore, with the definitive loss of the supernatural and intellectual vitality of modern man. Without the spiritual and intellectual life, the type of man-stomach must arise, the bourgeois, surrendering the whole of his mind, his heart, and his forces to economics.

Hence, at the end of the 18th century, the hour of the economy strikes, of a greedy economy, for which Luther prepared man (see note 1 at the end of the book), of a rational or mechanical economy, for which man was prepared by Descartes; of a liberal or individual economy, for which Rousseau prepared him.

2 Marcel Malcor, "L'économie contemporaine : travail, assurances, capitalisme," *Nova et Vetera* 6, no. 2 (April–June 1931): 122–158.

The understanding (the soul, the form) that man will form of the economy will be one of a mechanical structure, removed from human supervision (Descartes) with unlimited individual expansion (Rousseau) destined to multiply profit infinitely (Luther). In simpler words: a huge machine, in the hands of the individual, moved by the infinite concupiscence for profit.

THE ESSENCE OF CAPITALISM: MATERIAL ELEMENTS

We could say that this form of the economy found in the material conditions of that time a body that sustained this form, which in turn seemed to be made on purpose for such a body.

Thanks to the physical-mathematical sciences, the domination of the mechanical laws that govern the movement of the universe was achieved, and with this, the practical conquest of the world. On everyone's lips are the praises of the technical transformations brought about by the smelting of minerals in coal ovens in 1738, the production of cast iron in 1750, and the application of the machinery to the cotton and wool industry in 1760, precisely in the colossal industries of Lancashire. In this way, machinery conformed to the mechanical understanding that Descartes had made of the economy.

At the same time that machines dizzyingly and with mathematical regularity increased production possibilities in Europe, the agricultural state of the world opened an unlimited market to European industry. It is easy to imagine that a nascent industry, faced with huge and unlimited markets, would also demand unlimited production. Thus, the old customs barriers that opposed free circulation of goods, the regulations that limited production, and the moral and political disciplines that restricted private initiatives, were demolished.

The unlimited market thus offered a favorable material condition for Rousseau's liberal understanding of the economy.

The increase of the speculation of high finance, represented, as a paradigmatic case, by Mayer Rothschild, at the same time that credit will accelerate the capacity of machinery and the limitlessness of the market, will provide a propitious condition for the instinct for profit that has been opened in man since the Protestant Reformation.

The material conditions of the world conform to its formal conditions. Everything is ready, at the end of the 18th century, for liberal capitalism to emerge, just as now, in the last gasps of capitalism, the world, both because of its material and formal conditions, is ready to plunge into a gigantic anarchy.

DEFINITION OF CAPITALISM

Hence, we can define capitalism: it is an economic system that seeks the unlimited increase of profit by the application of mechanical economic laws.

Capitalism is any system that seeks unlimited profit, for which reason it wants unlimited production and consumption. It is defined, then, with the same formula used by the Angelic Doctor to condemn any business that seeks profit as its end: "the greed for gain, which knows no limit and tends to infinity" (ST II-II, q. 77, a. 4).

This is a definition that applies both to liberalism and Marxism. Both are imperialists; both intend to speed up economic growth in order to obtain the maximum yield and impose economic happiness on this earth, which should not be an inhabitable valley of tears as Christianity desired (as they claim), but rather a comfortable paradise.

But while liberalism concentrates wealth in the oligarchy of billionaires, Marxist greed accumulates it in the oligarchy of a proletarian minority that has become the State.

In this identical generic configuration, however, there are specific differences, because liberalism arrives at unfair concentration starting from individual wealth and unlimited freedom, whereas Marxism implants it by virtue of collectivist property.

In addition, while liberalism, by virtue of Cartesian influence, makes human work a purely mechanical operation, Marxism (theoretically) makes it into an irreducible element of a biological nature. This discovery of the biological character of work is symptomatic, because it heralds a new economy; it is also a disastrous economy, if man is not purified of his instinct for avarice, because then a proletarian tyranny will be established, as in Russia; however, it will be beneficent or Catholic, if it is purified.

Having exposed the nature of capitalism and quickly indicating its two main species, we are going to formulate its criticism, which will be preferentially directed at liberal capitalism.

CAPITALISM IS UNECONOMIC

Let us omit the fact that an economy governed by the concupiscence for profit as a fundamental law must turn out to be a Moloch that devours the economic welfare of the worker, which turns out to be a vile merchandise subjected to the swings of the market:

- It is a devourer of the consumer's concerns, since consumers do not enter into account except insofar as they allow the increase of production, and with it, the increase of profit (for this reason, as a general rule, it is assumed that they are allotted items that are superfluous or of poor quality, at relatively high prices);
- It devours the producer, who must live feverishly increasing his production and improving technical

tools, if he does not want to succumb to industrial competition;

- It devours the merchant, who must submit to the feverish dynamism of the consumer governed by the infinite fickleness of whim and the increase of industrial novelties, without having time to sell off his outdated stocks. The system is also the devourer of the financier, who must go on the hunt for the consumer, the producer, and the merchant, in order to bewilderingly increase, without rest, the productivity of his money.

Again, let us overlook all these delusional disorders, and let us only observe that capitalism, precisely by virtue of its capitalist essence, that is, its concupiscence for profit, carries in its entrails its own ruin without ever being able, even for an instant, to provide for man's economic well-being. In other words: it is essentially anti-economic.

Indeed, we can define it as: "the increase of profit due to the increase of production and consumption." Now then, as long as the limit that balances production with consumption is not reached, as long as there are unlimited markets open to production, it is clear that the unbridled increase of machinery and credit is favorable to the development of a capitalist economy, or, better said, to its numbness, like that of certain tumors that seem full of health. However, once production comes to balance the possibility of consumption (note well, I say possibility), liberal capitalism is dead. This is because, in order for it to continue living, it would be necessary to give an equal increase to consumption as to production, which is impossible, since production can increase 25% to 40% per year.

It has died: because if it can't speed up production, it can't speed up profit; and since this constitutes its essence, once consumption feels saturated, it must break up and disintegrate.

This is the meaning of the current crisis of capitalism—its definitive crisis.

Some will ask: how is it possible to speak of saturation, of balance between production and consumption, if today what can be consumed is in fact not consumed and there are immense riches to exploit and enormous comforts to achieve?

This objection has been anticipated when it was said: "balance the *possibility* of consumption," because capitalism has died not when what is produced is consumed, but rather what can be consumed; that is to say, that capitalism has not had and will not have, even for an instant, the fleeting consolation of fully satisfying consumption. And this is in the essence of capitalism.

Indeed, in capitalism, production and, even better, the financing of production, have primacy over consumption; hence, the greatest production must be sought at all costs, subordinating consumption to it. Thus, it is more profitable for production, in the period of non-saturation, not to ensure the worker a fair salary, the necessary means of subsistence, because in this way more productive wealth is available; then, in that time the immense multitude is subjected to the law of hunger. This is the story of liberal capitalism in the 19th century. On the other hand, when saturation has been reached, since production must be violently curtailed, there is a forced unemployment, and then arises the situation that our eyes contemplate today: enormous wealth, *capable* of feeding, clothing, and entertaining the whole human race and yet, on the other hand, an immense multitude submerged in misery, unable to consume because they do not have the means of acquisition.

Later, capitalism succumbs without ever ensuring the economic well-being of the human race.

This is because capitalism is essentially futuristic. It can claim to be an economy that is liberating for human life, because it hopes to be *for everyone in the future*, although in the meantime it is only for the benefit of a few. It is the same language and the same method of Soviet capitalism. However, this future, this tomorrow, can never come, because that impossibility is found in its essence. There is a profound contrast between Capitalism and the economy advocated by Christ in the Sermon on the Mount.

"Strive to get rich," says Capitalism, "only that counts." "Do not worry," says Eternal Wisdom instead, "about your life and what you will eat, or about your body and what you will wear. . . . Notice the ravens: they do not sow or reap; they have neither storehouse nor barn, yet God feeds them. . . . Notice how the flowers grow" (Lk 12:22-27).

Capitalism is busy, accumulating for tomorrow.

Instead, Jesus Christ tells us: "Do not worry about tomorrow; tomorrow will take care of itself. Sufficient for a day is its own evil" (Mt 6:34).

These are the words of Jesus Christ, which are not just pious advice. They express the law of economic life. The economy must think first of all about the needs of the present. What should be produced today is what is needed to be consumed today. This is because if, driven by greed, what is needed for the whole year is produced today, and one works like this every day, with the purpose of increasing profit, it will happen that today it will not be consumed so as not to reduce the production that is reserved for tomorrow (capitalism during the 19th century with starvation wages), and tomorrow, because production will have to stop to liquidate the stored stocks; and when production is stopped there will be no wages, with which there will be no possibility of consumption (capitalism in its heyday).[3]

GREED, THE ESSENCE OF CAPITALISM

Whatever its species, there is an essential perversity in capitalism, since this is a system founded on a capital vice

3 See note 2 at the end of the book.

which theologians call avarice. It seeks the unlimited increase of wealth as if it were an end in itself, as if its mere possession constituted man's happiness.

As the Angelic Doctor teaches:

> It is impossible for man's happiness to consist in wealth. For wealth is twofold, as the Philosopher says (*Polit.* i, 3), viz., natural and artificial. Natural wealth is that which serves man as a remedy for his natural wants: such as food, drink, clothing, vehicles, dwellings, and such like, while artificial wealth is that which is not a direct help to nature, as money, but is invented by the art of man, for the convenience of exchange, and as a measure of things salable.
>
> Now it is evident that man's happiness cannot consist in natural wealth. For wealth of this kind is sought for the sake of something else, viz., as a support of human nature: consequently it cannot be man's last end, rather is it ordained to man as to its end. Wherefore in the order of nature, all such things are below man, and made for him, according to Psalm 8: *Thou hast subjected all things under his feet* (8).
>
> And as to artificial wealth, it is not sought save for the sake of natural wealth; since man would not seek it except because, by its means, he procures for himself the necessaries of life.[c]

Now, says Aquinas, if both natural and artificial riches have the purpose of satisfying the material needs of man, according to the conditions of each one, their acquisition is only good to the extent that it serves to satisfy these needs;

c ST I-II, q. 2, a. 1.

hence the possession and production of these goods must be regulated.[d] If this measure is broken and one wants to retain and possess them without any limitation, a sin called avarice is committed, which consists of "it is an immoderate love of having possessions" (ST II-II, q. 118, a. 2).

It is precisely this concupiscence of profit that constitutes the essence of the modern economy. It is not that greed has only existed in the modern economy; there have always been greedy persons, and the Holy Spirit says through the mouth of Solomon that "all things obey money" (Eccles. 10:19); but never as in the modern economy has this perverse impulse that nests in the sinful flesh of man been organized in an economic system; no one has made a sin into a Babel-like construction like the modern economy.

Since greed is a capital vice with many daughters—according to the Angelic Doctor (II-II, q. 118, a. 8)—capitalism has erected with it a progeny of sins, systems that economists call economic laws.

"*Since avarice consists in a needless love of riches, there is a double disorder in it: either these goods are unduly retained or they are acquired illicitly. There is disorder in its retention, in the case of inhumanity or hardening of the heart, when the heart does not soften with mercy in the presence of the needy,* and thus capitalism, like all misers, closes its heart to the miseries of the poor. Capital, an anonymous monster with a thousand powers and without any responsibility, is not interested in charity, or piety, or even equity itself, nor does it even believe that it has duties towards the individuals whom it employs. In any case, the duty [of capitalism] is of the same order as that with respect to the production of capital, namely: a scrupulous and methodical maintenance, as long as this maintenance produces business: the stopping of production or

d It is not clear where Meinvielle finds this textually in Aquinas.

unemployment when finances demand it or prefer it."[4] *There is also disorder in avarice, because riches are acquired either with disordered affection or by resorting to illicit means. This is because greed breeds a "morbid restlessness and a feverish preoccupation with the superfluous," which makes Ecclesiastes (5:9), say "A covetous man shall not be satisfied with money"*; thus, capitalism, dynamic, vertiginous, insatiable, uses every minute ("time is money") to increase profit, and with it, production and consumption; life is a tireless race in pursuit of gold; wealth is not sought to live but lives to get rich. How far we are from the Catholic economy, governed by the procurement of daily bread!

In the same way, avarice also gives rise to other vices like so many other daughters: violence, falsehood, perjury, fraud, and treachery. Capitalism is guilty of violence, because, with its hunger for increased wealth, it devours small industry and small property; it is false, because it promises the freedom of the entire human race and each day plunges it more deeply into misery, since concentration of wealth on one side corresponds to desolation on the other; capitalism commits the sin of perjury, when falsehood is joined to an oath, and capitalism signs its deception with credit, as will be explained in the 4th chapter; it commits sins of fraud, because with the credit or loan at interest it seizes the savings of the human race and manages them as if it were an owner, because it subjects the worker to the law of hunger, and because it ensures bad and expensive consumption; lastly, capitalism commits the sin of treachery, because it annihilates the human person, making man a mere individual, a simple wheel in the gigantic machinery of the economic edifice. It tears apart the family, crowding men and women in factories as if they were a herd of animals, and it destroys education with the standardization of

4 Marcel Malcor, "L'économie contemporaine : le crédit ou l''usure'," *Nova et Vetera* 6, no. 3 (July 1931): 265–284.

the school and the suppression of learning.

In short, since capitalism is like the eruption of a whole family of sins, it is the kingdom of Mammon. This critique applies to both liberal and Marxist capitalism.

THE CATHOLIC ECONOMY

On the other hand, the economy, the only possible economy, is founded on the virtue that Saint Thomas calls liberality, which teaches us the good use of the goods of this world granted for our sustenance (ST II-II, q. 117).

Should artificial and natural wealth be produced and accumulated just for the sake of it? Certainly not. These are things intended for the benefit of man, for his use; let's say simply: "for consumption." They are goods, and not simply things to the extent that they take advantage or can take advantage of man. Hence, due to the demands of the economy itself, the entire economic process must be oriented towards consumption. Hence there is a double anti-economic failure in capitalism, whatever its kind, because goods are consumed to be produced and they are produced in order to make a profit. Finance regulates production, and production regulates consumption.

And the goods, what are they consumed for? In other words, the entirety of the economic process, to where is it directed? To satisfy the necessities of man's bodily life. Since it does not have an end in itself, but rather its integrity is required to ensure man's spiritual life, which culminates in the act of love for God, the entire economy must be at the service of man so that he is at the service of God.

"Saint Thomas teaches that in order to lead a moral life, to develop in the life of virtues, man needs a minimum of well-being and material security. This teaching means," says Maritain, "that misery is socially, as Leon Bloy and Péguy have clearly seen, a kind of hell. It also means that the social conditions that place the majority of men in the near occasion of sin, demanding a kind of heroism from those who want to practice the law of God, are conditions that in strict justice must be relentlessly denounced and that one must strive to change."[5,e]

In his *Summa Contra Gentiles* (SCG III, c. 37), Saint Thomas has explained the place of the economy in a hierarchy of values:

> All other human operations seem to be directed to this as their end. For perfect contemplation requires that the body should be disencumbered, and to this effect are directed all the products of art that are necessary for life. Moreover, it requires freedom from the disturbance caused by the passions, which is achieved by means of the moral virtues and prudence; and freedom from external disturbance, to which all the regulations of the civil life are directed. So that, if we consider the matter rightly, we shall see that all human occupations are brought into the service of those who contemplate the truth.

As long as this hierarchy of values is not accepted and in use, capitalism will not be overcome, because either God is served or Mammon, the god of wealth.

THE ECONOMY AS ETHICS

From the foregoing it follows that the economy is a sort of ethics (against Descartes' mechanical understanding) that has as its specific objective the procurement of the material goods useful to man. I say goods, that is: that they correspond to the demands of human nature, not to its whims or concupiscences. Hence, all those things that are left over, once

5 Maritain, *Religion et culture*.

e Trans. from Maritain, "Religion and Culture," 27.

the needs of the state itself are satisfied, are superfluous and are not good if they are kept accumulated or used to satisfy the thirst for pleasures. There is a serious obligation, as we will establish in the next lesson, to allow all the members of the social community to participate in the use of these goods so that they become useful goods for man, that is: human material goods, which should only be used insofar as they lead to the rational fulfillment and supernatural destiny of man. We must make use of wealth as children of God *that we call ourselves and that we are.*

Hence the economy is a part of prudence, as Saint Thomas teaches (ST I-II, q. 51, a. 3), which has as its object the right ordering of human actions aimed at procuring self-support or that of the family or of the society.

Since in the law of grace in which we live there can be no perfect virtue—as Aquinas teaches—but by ordering everything to the "God who is to be loved above all things," it is necessary that prudence, and with it the economy, are perfectly subordinated to charity, which is the most excellent of virtues, and without which there can be no true virtue.

From what has been said it follows that "economic laws are not purely physical laws like those of mechanics or chemistry, but rather laws of human action which imply moral values. Justice, liberality, and ordered love of neighbor are an essential part of the economic reality. The oppression of the poor and wealth taken as an end in itself are not only prohibited by individual morality, but are also things that are economically bad, which go against the very end of the economy, because this end is a human end."[6,f]

For this reason, the justification of the economic elements and values must be sought in the demands of human action,

6 Maritain, *Religion et culture*, 46.

f Trans. from Maritain, "Religion and Culture," 26–27.

and its morality, its intrinsic morality, will be the consequences of its beneficial effects for man.

TRANSCENDENCE OF THE CATHOLIC ECONOMY

I don't know if the fundamental opposition of the economy (because only the truly human economy can be called simply economy) and the modern economy or capitalism has been clearly delineated. One is founded on a sin, and the other rests on a virtue. One, like all sin, under wonderful disguises, enslaves man, because whoever commits sin is a slave to sin, according to the Apostle. The other, humbly, without ostentation, frees him, because the truth sets us free, as Christ taught.

If the modern economy is born of sin, it is essentially perverse and nefarious. There may be many good material elements in it, but their makeup is intrinsically diabolical.

Hence the economic doctrine of the Church, born of a virtue, is a doctrine that is infinitely above all other economic doctrines, whether they be called socialist or liberal. It cannot and should not be compared with them. It is not in the middle of them. Like the peak of a tall mountain, it collects, transcending, all the points of truth contained in the different economic schools; because, just as there is no absolute evil or error, so every school, no matter how delusional, has within it many adulterated truths. For example, liberalism insists on the individual character of the possession of earthly goods, socialism insists on the social character, and fascism wants to balance both. However, it is only the Church, which finds its support in the eternity of heaven, that can obtain a true balance between man and wealth, because incorporated into Christ, and through Christ united with God, she can submit wealth to man and man to God. Man is placed in the middle, between riches and God. He can never rule. Therefore, if he does not want to come to God, if he refuses to accept God's rule, he must fall under the rule of riches. Either God or

Mammon: you cannot serve two lords. But man must serve: if he refuses God's paternal rule, he will fall under the bondage of the golden calf.

There are only two truly opposite economies: the Christian one, which uses riches to ascend to God, and the modern or capitalist one (be it liberal or Marxist), which abandons God to enslave itself in wealth.

It seems that divine mercy, pitying man's terrible fate, man who has lost the supernatural paradise and lives in a terrestrial hell, wants at this time to free us from capitalist oppression. This is the meaning of the deep crisis that weighs upon the world.

But there are two ways for liberation to take place. If man understands God's plan, the God who wants to free us from bourgeois oppression, from slavery to gold, man gives himself over to divine desires and, in a spirit of penance, renounces what is superfluous and, to atone for his perverse greed, deprives himself even of what is necessary; the Lord, who forgave Nineveh, will return to man the meaning of economy and, with it, the meaning of life. Liberation will then have been accomplished in the peace of the Lord.

If, on the other hand, he does not understand God's plan, or pretends not to understand it, the Lord will free him, it is true, but after purifying him in a frightful catastrophe of terror and anarchy.

Chapter 2

The Production of the Earth

IN THE PREVIOUS CHAPTER we discovered in real time the essential and disastrous perversion of any economy that, like capitalism, is intrinsically ruled by the desire for profit. Since this is an insatiable instinct, infinitely vertiginous, dynamic, accelerating, it rebels against any restraint, and for this reason it entails a radical inversion of all human values and even economic values themselves. It inverts human values, because instead of putting the economy at the service of man's bodily life, so that he can thus achieve the integrity of his intellectual and spiritual life and place himself at the service of God (the only Lord who deserves full obedience), the modern understanding of economics absorbs all the spiritual and material energies of man. It places them at the mercy of the gigantic economic edifice, around which everyone throughout the world—from the last unemployed person to the powerful financier—is obliged to prostrate himself in a religious dance.

It produces an inversion of economic values themselves: because instead of using money as simply a means of exchange that facilitates the distribution and dissemination of natural wealth, it becomes precisely the opposite, that is, a last end, with a powerful force of attraction that concentrates more money in a few hands, and with it natural wealth as well.

The capitalist economy is arranged in such a way that everything contributes to the multiplication of gold: wealth and credit serve to multiply gold; if there is trade, it is in order to multiply gold; if there is production, it is in order to trade and thereby multiply gold; if there is consumption, it is in order to produce more and thereby trade more and be able to increase gold even more. Thus, life is a perpetual dance around gold, which, to top it off, no one sees because it sleeps in the mysterious caverns of the big banks.

In this situation, consumption, which should be the proximate regulating end of the entire economic process, ultimately comes to be subordinated to production, trade, and finance; on the other hand, finance, which should occupy the last place since it is purely a means, takes first place as the end that regulates everything.

HIERARCHY OF PRODUCTION

This unhealthy acceleration must at the same time cause a profound upheaval in particular economic phenomena, such as that of *production*.

Without entering into metaphysical considerations that might seem profound, let us apply common sense and ask: what is the purpose of the production of goods? Why does man engage in work and produce? No doubt in order to obtain goods that he can consume. This does not mean that he should only produce what he can consume each day. Not at all. He can and should produce more, save what he does not consume, and form a stable patrimony that will ensure life for him and his family in the future and that will be passed down to his heirs. However, even that which he does not immediately consume, he produces in anticipation of the consumption that he will need tomorrow without being able to produce it then. Therefore, it will always be true that he produces in order to consume. And what are the first goods that man needs to consume? What are the first goods that he needs: to have rest and joy, to live in a suitable house, to dress, or to eat? No doubt the first of all is to eat, and then to dress, and then to have a suitable house, and finally to enjoy honest pastimes. Since the land is what almost directly provides us with what is necessary to eat, dress, and live, whereas industry preferentially supplies us with what is superfluous, it follows that, in an orderly economic regime, the production of the land and its riches must have primacy over industrial production, that is, country life over urban life.

In other words: exactly the opposite of what happens and must necessarily happen in the modern economy. In its essence, the capitalist economy is pure increase. The production of the land and the consumption of its products are removed from that increase: for example, it is not possible to obtain wheat in a few days or in a few hours, or to consume 10 kilos of bread instead of one. In contrast, the production of superfluous goods can increase indefinitely, because it is always possible to create new superfluous needs and to satisfy them infinitely. Hence, the capitalist economy, by its very essence, feels driven to the phenomenon "contra naturam" (that violates natural demands) of making industry, the factory, the normal type of production and instead envisioning agriculture as a trailer dragged by industry. Henry Ford has had the frankness to confess it when he considers agriculture as an "auxiliary or subsidiary" industry, according to his own words.[1,a]

1 In Henry Ford, *Ma vie et mon oeuvre; Aujourd'hui et demain,* 230; cited by Marcel Malcor, "L'économie contemporaine," *Nova et Vetera* 4, no. 1 (January–March 1929): 49–75.

a The translation follows the French cited by Meinvielle, but the

This disorder of production must engender phenomena that are typical of capitalism, for instance, the production and consumption of an article are greater the more useless it is. Take, for example, the American woman: in 1925, on average she spent three times more on cosmetics than she did on bread, and now, in the midst of the economic crisis,[b] we see that, with an evident underconsumption of food and clothing, there is a splurge on cigarettes, entertainment, newspapers, alcohol, and the like; then, the phenomenon of human crowding in the so-called big cities, where life is rickety and miserable but full of entertainment, while the fields remain deserted. These are the same fields, possessed by and of benefit to a few owners, who amuse themselves in the city's harem, in which the tenant farmers are consumed in the sweat that yields nothing but misery; lastly, these are the fields of industrialized and commercialized agricultural exploitation, in such a way that it does not ensure a decent life for the farmer.

This total inversion of the hierarchy of production, this absorption that the market and industry make of the land and its production provoke a radical upheaval of the farm itself. It is necessary to be convinced that the problem of farming has no solution in a capitalist economy, in an economy that is driven by greed as its own end. Herein lies the disastrous error of all those who, seeing the anguish of property and agricultural exploitation, want to remedy it by appealing to an

original is presumably the following: after discussing how to modify the farming industry, Ford notes "Farming then shows up as the part-time job it really is, and straight farming will eventually have to be considered only as a side issue. Farming is no exception to what might be called the rule of nature that one month's work will not support twelve months of living. The real problem of farming is to find something in addition to farming for the farmer to earn a living at. That is the plain, rough truth" (Henry Ford, *Today and Tomorrow* (Boca Raton, FL: CRC Press, 2003), 202).

b Recall the original version of Meinvielle's text was published in 1936, during the Great Depression.

equitable distribution of land or solidarity cooperation, without first straightening out the crooked or inverted order of economic life.

Even if an ideal distribution of the land were made and an equally ideal use of it was implemented, absolutely nothing would be remedied until the modern understanding of the economy itself was reformed and the meaning of the natural economic hierarchy restored. This is because, as I have said before, the economic chaos of the countryside, which, between us, goes beyond all measure, is the result of industrial, commercial, and financial causes, and the problem has no real solution if the land and products of nature do not recover their regulatory function of production, a task which the very nature of economic reality has assigned them. This is an observation that may seem impractical to many but that can be verified by the simple fact of the crisis: a bountiful harvest and first-class livestock that cannot be placed on world markets at an advantageous price is enough to plunge into misery and starvation the entirety of the rural farming population.

THE DOMESTIC AND RURAL TYPE OF PRODUCTION

So that this simple fact that is adduced only as a mere example does not serve to diminish the scope of this observation, note that the chaos of the countryside is permanent because its life is permanently attracted and as if magnetized by the anemic life of the city, because its production is dragged by industrial and commercial production; obviously, however, the mess will be greater when in turn there is a disorder in industry and commerce as well.

When the land loses its own life and is linked to industrialism and mercantilism, the uprising of the farmers is imminent; the landowners who live in the city can hurry to the slaughter.

It will be helpful to remember what happened in the 4th century in North Africa:

In the 3rd and 4th centuries, Numidia and Byzacena supplied olive oil to the civilized world; anticipating modern formulas, they established specialized export-oriented farming and industry. It is clear that these are two reasons why the larger properties, which were better organized and equipped with better resources, especially from the point of view of foreign trade, ended up swallowing the small ones. As a result, in the fourth century, Africa was divided into a few farms. The owner-farmer has disappeared, the serfs are less numerous; the settlers or free countrymen of yesteryear, reduced to a true proletariat, must pay dearly for their bread in these properties where everything is sacrificed to industrial exploitation. Impersonal troops of wage earners invade the fields.

One fine day, an agrarian revolution wiped out a whole class of landowners, and luxury towns, towns of owners like Lambesa, Tirngad, Aquae Regiae, Thisdrus, all of a sudden disappeared. The settlers divided up the land, and the weakened power passed into the hands of the vandals, as they are called.[2]

It is not my intent to instill fear in anyone. I only want to make it clear that an ordered production of the land requires that economic production is not *primarily* (I stress: primarily) neither financier, nor mercantilist, nor industrialist.

Production from the land should be more widespread and should be preferred to industrial production. Within the same land, production must first be domestic and only later mercantile.

If no one, obsessed by the monster of capitalist *progress* suffers scandal, I will write the word: economic production must be preferentially *patriarchal*. By this, I mean to say that what must be the predominant sort of possession is the type of

2 Malcor, "L'économie contemporaine : travail, assurances, capitalisme."

plot of land on which a modest family can live frugally, and in production, the dominant type should be of domestic and farm products, so that the common type of family, being able to produce such things in their own house, is never seen to fall into misery. I have said *preferentially*: indeed, there must be cities and industries, even with salaried personnel, but they must not dominate; such things, like large-scale farming, should take a back seat. Therefore, if we are considering how to bring about the general outline of an orderly, *humane* regime of economic production, it must be *rural* as opposed to urban, *domestic* as opposed to mercantile.

Let the glorifiers of the capitalist economy think that all their dithyrambs to Progress, to Industry, to the City, dissolve like soap balloons, when at the foot of these colossi, raised with the sweat of the poor, they contemplate the spiritual and material misery of the starving proletariat and the ruin and uncertainties of the tenant farmer in the fields. If a certain so-called progress must serve to enslave man, supplying him with enjoyments that he does not need and depriving him of the spiritual and material bread that sustains him, may Progress in good time drown. As perhaps some naive socialist imagines that the ideal would be to raise up the proletariat and seat it in the feast of the bourgeois paradise, it is good to remind them not to delude themselves. This is because the stomach paradise of the bourgeois has arisen precisely because it is bourgeois: in other words, because an economic understanding was in force that favored individual enrichment.

If the economic understanding had been statist, collectivist, or socialist, one of two alternatives would have taken place: or compulsory labor would have been implemented, and then perhaps a powerful collective wealth would have been achieved, but at the cost of slavery (which would also be collective, as in Russia), or man would have been left completely free, and nothing would be produced, not even to eat, because if the collective produces and feeds, there is no need for the individual to worry.

For this reason, without euphemisms, without zealous practical solutions, I say that if you do not want capitalist slavery or Marxist slavery, you must seek a patriarchal, rural, and domestic economy.

Let's be clear—I am not saying that this is possible in the near future, nor that it is of immediate practical application. It simply could not be, because this present economic structure is determined by liberalism, just as liberal and Marxist capitalism have been engendered by the bourgeois or proletarian greed, and today the instinct of greed is more virulent than ever.

However, I do say that it is the only economic configuration that can free us from oppression, be it capitalist or Marxist.

THE COMMON USE OF EXTERNAL GOODS

All of this doctrine regarding the hierarchy of the factors of production and regarding the need for a patriarchal type of economy is a corollary of the admirable teaching of Aristotle and Saint Thomas on *the use of material goods.*

Man arrives in the world, and finds himself faced with an infinity of external goods: the earth with its immense wealth of plants and animals, of fish in the water, and of birds in the skies. For whom and for what are these goods? God *has put all things at his feet,* answers the Psalmist in Psalm 8 (v. 7).

So everything is at man's service; everything is so that man can use it, that is, to eat, dress, build his house, and enjoy human delight in family life.

However, everything is for man: but, for which man? Are they for those of a race, a nation, a city, a social class? Not at all. Everyone, even the humblest of human beings, has the right to *use,* I say *use* and not precisely possess, what he and his family need for a human life. No one can be excluded. Indeed, an economic system that does not permanently assure all families what is necessary for human subsistence would be a disastrous, perverse, unjust regime. For this reason, Saint Thomas, following Aristotle, says: "The second thing that is competent to man with regard to external things is their use. In this respect man ought to possess external things, not as his own, but as common."[3,c]

The reason is clear: every man has the right to live in a family; hence, he has the right to the means that assure him of subsistence for his human family. However, since these means are external goods, every man has the right to external goods that ensure his subsistence and that of his family. Pay close attention as to how I now determine the minimum of what a man should *use*. This minimum is the human subsistence of the family. The key word is *human*: therefore, it means something more than just what is needed to eat and be clothed. It is a certain permanent human well-being. It might be a *poor* state, that is, that the family does not have superfluous riches to dispose of (that is, disposable income), but that state must never be *miserable*. God does not want anyone's misery. *An economic regime or system that sets man in misery is an unjust system, one condemned by God.*

For this motive both Socialism and Capitalism are condemned; by virtue of their very essence, both the one and the other permanently set man in a state of misery. Capitalism does this as it concentrates the ownership and use of goods in the hands of a few lucky millionaires and leaves the multitude condemned to live (rather, I say, to die) on a precarious and sporadic salary. Socialism does the same, because it also brutally concentrates property in the hands of the state, from where it follows that the multitude will often be deprived of its use. It is true that socialism imagines the appropriation by the

3 ST II-II, q. 66, a. 2 ad 7; *Pol.* II, 4.

c The citation should be simply ST II-II, q. 66, a. 2, *corpus*.

state of the goods produced in order to later distribute them and make them available for consumption by all men; but, as Aristotle and Saint Thomas have already seen with a penetrating gaze, such a regime, in addition to violating the just freedom of all and not taking into account the inequality of individual natures, would bring, as a logical consequence, the insufficiency of production. This is because, as daily experience proves, what pertains to everyone to do, nobody does. If everyone must produce collectively, very little would be produced.

Hence, in the same article in which he establishes the common use of external goods, Saint Thomas affirms and demonstrates the need for private property (ST II-II, q. 66, a. 2).

Thus, considering the question of whether it is lawful for man to possess something as his own, he answers:

> I answer that, two things are competent to man in respect of exterior things. One is the power to procure and dispense them, and in this regard it is lawful for man to possess property. Moreover this is necessary to human life for three reasons. First, because every man is more careful to procure what is for himself alone than that which is common to many or to all: since each one would shirk the labor and leave to another that which concerns the community, as happens where there is a great number of servants. Second, because human affairs are conducted in more orderly fashion if each man is charged with taking care of some particular thing himself, whereas there would be confusion if everyone had to look after any one thing indeterminately. Third, because a more peaceful state is ensured to man if each one is contented with his own. Hence it is to be

> observed that quarrels arise more frequently where there is no division of the things possessed. The second thing that is competent to man with regard to external things is their use. In this respect man ought to possess external things, not as his own, but as common, so that, to wit, he is ready to communicate them to others in their need. Hence the Apostle says [1 Tm 6:17, 18]: *Charge the rich of this world . . . to give easily, to communicate to others*, etc.[d]

PRIVATE PROPERTY

Thus we see that the common use of external goods founds and justifies private property, as Pius XI affirms in his marvelous *Quadragesimo Anno*, when he says:

> [Leo and those theologians who have taught under the guidance and authority of the Church] have always unanimously maintained that nature, rather the Creator Himself, has given man the right of private ownership not only that individuals may be able to provide for themselves and their families *but also that the goods which the Creator destined for the entire family of mankind may through this institution truly serve this purpose.* All this can be achieved in no wise except through the maintenance of a certain and definite order.[e]

If you want to understand the problem of private property, you must first understand the common use of goods, or that is, in other words, *the right to existence* that pertains to every member of the human family. The right of private property is a

d ST II-II, q. 66, a 2.

e Pius XI, "Quadragesimo Anno" (Encyclical, Rome, Italy, May 15, 1931), 45.

necessary means, but a means, whose *end* is to ensure the *common* use of exterior goods (common use: which does not mean that everyone must use anything and everything but rather that no one should go without that minimum that is necessary to live).

Economic liberalism, which makes the right to property all-encompassing, cannot be effectively avoided if this right to property is not derived from the common use of goods. The doctrine of Catholic theologians on the right of everyone who is in dire need to take what he needs for himself and his family is also based on this doctrine: "It is lawful for a man to succor his own need by means of another's property, by taking it either openly or secretly: nor is this properly speaking theft or robbery."[4]

The right of the State to limit and regulate private property in such a way that it effectively reaches its common destination is also based on the same doctrine. This is because if private property is to ensure the common use of external goods, the State, whose mission is to promote the common good, must regulate it for that purpose.

Pius XI has recalled this doctrine in *Quadragesimo Anno* when he writes:

> Therefore, public authority, under the guiding light always of the natural and divine law, can determine more accurately upon consideration of the true requirements of the common good, what is permitted and what is not permitted to owners in the use of their property. Moreover, Leo XIII wisely taught "that God has left the limits of private possessions to be fixed by the industry of men and institutions of peoples." That history proves ownership, like other elements of social

4 ST II-II, q. 66, a. 7.

> life, to be not absolutely unchanging, We once declared as follows: "What divers forms has property had, from that primitive form among rude and savage peoples, which may be observed in some places even in our time, to the form of possession in the patriarchal age; and so further to the various forms under tyranny (We are using the word tyranny in its classical sense); and then through the feudal and monarchial forms down to the various types which are to be found in more recent times.[f]

In this determination of property, the State's action must be such that, far from abolishing private property, it tends to guarantee it and make it effective, so that every family, as far as possible, has its own stable heritage that is passed down from generation to generation.

The ideal of government policy should be to secure *family property* for urban and peasant families, and then to protect it with effective legislation. This is precisely the opposite of liberal and socialist politics; they are determined to destroy the family, be it with disastrous laws that threaten the indissolubility of the marriage bond or by means of the standardized and "imbecilized" public education which diminish parental authority and education. They can also do this with laws on the division of the inheritance, inspired by the Napoleonic Code, or with the imposition of mortgages on the family's own property. If you want an ordering of property and agricultural life, it is necessary to restore the patrimony of the family. What is a family patrimony? It is a good in which successive owners are invested because it is perpetuated in the same family line, without any division. It is a good that is

f Pius XI, "Quadragesimo Anno," 49.

inalienable, cannot be seized, and which cannot be mortgaged, recognized by Germanic law that Le Play calls family-lineage.[5]

To continue explaining what a healthy economic understanding requires of the production of the earth, I will say that once the family patrimony, the rural domain, which is like the organic cell of agricultural production, has been restored, it will be necessary to coordinate the work of the different families, that is, the small or medium-sized agricultural works, in such a way that it is not absorbed by the larger works or devoured by the powerful landowner. Cooperation is necessary, cooperation that will be able to protect the rights of the farmer in the natural economic concurrence: it will defend him against usurers by means of credit unions such as Cajas Raiffeisen. Cooperation will instruct him regarding the improvements that should be introduced for the crops; it will provide him with the convenient fertilizers and the instruments of production, especially the most expensive ones. It will free him from commercial oppression by consumer cooperatives, and will ensure the storage and sale of crops by production cooperatives. In a word: they will become true agricultural unions that provide for the common needs of farmers.

Obviously, all these measures will be completely useless if the government does not firmly prevent monopolies and speculation of international intermediaries. In my opinion, in reality we have reached a critical point, in which the power of speculation is almost indestructible, while the power of the State, due to democratic liberalism, is very weak, it is necessary to organize the land so that it is possible to satisfy the country's own needs in such a way that production first supplies the country before directing itself to the world market. This will obviously require a less mercantilist agricultural distribution, less lucrative but more abundant in

5 See René La Tour du Pin, *Vers un ordre social Chretien*.

natural goods. It is necessary to sponsor a mixed farm, agricultural-horticultural-poultry-livestock. Naturally, in our country, this means making it difficult for people to return to their normal indolence.

In this way, we would have the same excessive speculation of the monopolies, as well as the rhythm of the world market, which is frankly protectionist, suggesting a return to a patriarchal type of land production, of which I spoke before.

THE STATE CAN LIMIT PRIVATE PROPERTY

Previously I underscored that the common use of external goods justifies and regulates private property such that, as far as possible, every family should have an inalienable fixed patrimony. However, this has been present more as an end to which we should direct ourselves, although it can never be achieved perfectly. There will always be people who, either of their own free will or out of necessity, will not have their own plot of land. In the countryside, this will be the condition of the tenant or sharecropper. Both the leasing system and the sharecropping system are in themselves fair as long as the stipulated price is fair. However, we can say that generally the prices are exorbitant, because they are calculated for times of exceptional prosperity. In addition, it is a flagrant injustice (at least a social injustice, insofar as it goes against the common use of external goods) that the large landowners demand payment of their rents in these years of losses, even though the farmers find themselves in distress.

Although the leasing system as such is fair, an orderly production of the land requires that the cultivators are preferably the owners themselves. What happens in Argentina, that is, is that at least 70 percent of the land under cultivation is leased (and this in extremely disadvantageous conditions) and this reveals a deep disorder. It is not easy to point out the solution to this problem, but it is necessary to be convinced that a solution is necessary both for justice and for social peace. The farmer is patient, but everything has a limit, and it is not fair to abuse anyone's patience.

By virtue of its role as guardian of the common good, the State has the power to apply the solution that considers the good of all.

In order to show how far this power can go, and at the same time demonstrate in an example the limitation that the common use of external goods imposes on private property, I will briefly explain the energetic policy applied by the Popes in the fifteenth century against landowners and monopolists.

At the end of the fifteenth century, the *Agro romano,* a part of the countryside of Rome, was in a state of pitiful desolation, while in Rome there was an appalling shortage. The owners of the Roman agricultural lands preferred to let the land spontaneously produce grass for the grazing of wild animals than to force it on their own or tolerate that others would force it to bear fruit for the sustenance of men.

It was then that Pope Sixtus IV, in his famous bull *Inducit nos,* of March 19, 1476, empowered everyone in the territory of Rome to plow and cultivate, at the customary times, a third of any residence that they chose, whoever owned it, on the condition that they ask for permission, but with the power to farm even if they did not obtain permission, even if they paid a fee or rent to the owners.

As can be seen, in this case, the State, by virtue of its jurisdictional power or legal justice, without depriving the owners of their domain (as evidenced by the payment of rent), regulates it in such a way that the use and usufruct of the property is shared by all.

The Bull of Clement VII will more effectively demonstrate the extent of this power.

The result of the bull of Sixtus IV was that "very many dedicated themselves to farming," but since later the barons forbade their vassals to transport the harvested grain, in order to force them to sell it to them cheaply and then resell it, nobody wanted to continue farming. This is the case of the vulgar monopoly of Dreyfus, Bunge & Born, etc., already recorded by Aristotle back in his days.[g] What could the Pope do to remedy this situation?

He severely forbade all Roman barons, nobles, and any other persons: 1) To buy wheat and other grains from his own vassals, other than what was necessary for the use and support of his household; 2) To prevent the vassals from taking wheat and grain to Rome; and 3) That they themselves transport it to any place other than that city.

To give effect to the prohibition, the bull threatened that those who would not obey within 15 days of the promulgation of the bull would incur the sentence of excommunication, from which they could be absolved only by the Roman Pontiff, with express mention of the case, only when at the point of death, and with satisfaction expressly made. If they would still would not obey, after another 15 days they would be entirely deprived of their fiefdom, which would be confiscated for the benefit of the Apostolic Camera. If, six months after the last 15 days, they still refused to obey, then, *ipso jure*, they would be deprived of all the towns, lands, estates, fiefdoms, and rights, with the inability to recover them or possess others forever; the cities, towns, lands, estates, and rights will be fully incorporated into the Apostolic Camera.[6]

It is obviously not a question of proposing the application of this example to remedy our situation. The point is to show how far the State's power can go in the regulation of property.

---

6 See Narciso Noguer, *Cuestiones candentes sobre la propiedad y el socialismo.*

---

g It appears the Dreyfus reference refers to the Louis Dreyfus Company B.V. (LDC), also called the Louis-Dreyfus Group, since Léopold Louis-Dreyfus started as a farmer and grain merchant. Bunge & Born, now Bunge Limited, is a corporation founded in 1884 by Ernesto Bunge in Argentina. For a time, the company almost held a monopoly of cereal and grain exports.

That this regulation is such that if someone disobeys it, it can carry the penalty of losing that property itself. This is because, if we pay close attention, in the case cited, the Pope does not deprive anyone of property until after the owner has been convicted of a crime against social justice; it is a crime not to abide by the regulation of property imposed by the State in view of the common good.

Furthermore, note that the application of an energetic measure can be justified by the doctrine of the common use of goods, which authorizes those who are in dire need to take what belongs to others so as not to perish from misery. If a family can do just that, it seems that, if there are many families that find themselves in misery, because the only capital they have, the work of their hands, is worth zero (if there is unemployment, it is worth zero), the State itself must then take charge of the distribution of the goods that others possess superfluously.

A RADICAL COROLLARY SOLUTION TO THIS DOCTRINE

Perhaps the time has come, or is yet to come, for a firm regulation of private property. Today there is an unfair accumulation of goods in the hands of a few while the multitude is not simply in poverty, but rather in misery. This implies a social injustice and a serious threat to the social order. It is urgent to find a solution.

However, the State, whose mission is to ensure social justice, must remedy it by appealing to effective solutions. These must be such that they do not ignore property rights. The State must respect private property, and since it would be impossible, in the present case, to determine which assets were furtively acquired, it must refrain from attempting to determine it and must leave the assets in the hands of those where they are currently found.

Nonetheless, while respecting the current ownership, the State can and must seek a solution to the problem of unemployment and misery. To do this, it must make a comprehensive study of the current distribution of financial, commercial, industrial, and agricultural assets; it must examine the yield of these goods and their distribution to inquire why, even with this yield of wealth, there are thousands of families in the country that do not have the necessary subsistence.

Once these causes have been examined, and for this there is nothing better than consulting the economic forces of the country (workers, farmers, ranchers, land-owners, industrialists, etc.), it will energetically apply the solution that best corresponds to social justice, namely: *It is not possible that in this country, so rich in natural goods, sufficient for an immensely larger population, there are those who, by virtue of the social economic order, lacks the stable human subsistence to which they are entitled as members of the social community.*

The State will then impose as obligatory those measures that it deems necessary to achieve the realization of this social requirement, taking into account that it is not fair that there are thousands of families in misery while others enjoy an income of 5,000, 10,000, 20,000, 50,000, one hundred thousand, and two hundred thousand pesos monthly.

Government measures will not consist of depriving those who make these excessive profits of their property and wealth, but rather of forcing them to extend these benefits to the largest number of needy families, either by providing work, or with a better remuneration for work, or by delivering these benefits to the State so that it can distribute them among the needy families of the community.

If the holders of these productive wealth refuse, either due to selfishness or lack of social sense, to submit to these regulations, the government should not hesitate to punish them as violators of the social order; and there is no more efficacious punishment than to deprive them of their riches, according to the example of the Popes above mentioned.

A CONSIDERATION REGARDING OUR COUNTRY

In a country of the natural wealth of ours, there is no reason for there to be misery. If there is misery to be found, it is due exclusively to the poor management of our economic life, which is more an economy of profit than of subsistence. Our country has been and is exploited by foreigners as a factory. With the country structured as a production factory for foreigners, our well-being is at the mercy of the prices imposed on us by speculators. When these prices do not cover the cost, production stops, and as happens and must happen now, bankruptcy and the most appalling misery reign.

Where is the permanent solution that can save us from misery today and will do so in the future and that forms genuinely Argentine generations, rooted in our lands?

The solution is this: a total change of our economic structuring: that our economy ceases to be for profit, mercantilist, and becomes an economy of subsistence, of consumption.

Rural plots must be forged for families. Let families take root in the land; the rich in their ranches and the poor in their farms, country houses, or little lands. May they take root in their own soil to perpetuate themselves in it in robust and copious generations. And let them live on their land. How is it possible that today's farm workers, set in contact with the land, a fertile mother, suffer misery, if not because they work artificially "to sell" and not to live?

When the orientation of economic life is changed, families will grow fond of their own soil, and will not live in anguished shock like today's farm workers, victims of the speculator, who do not know what tomorrow will bring.

Once the rural domain has been restored, as I explained in the body of this chapter, the rural market must also be rebuilt, within a region, to enlighten and stimulate farmers. In Italy, there are experiments and experiences that have been undertaken that deserve to be applauded and imitated.

In addition, it is necessary to organize the entire productive life of our lands in national institutions in order to carry out, on the basis of the domestic and rural economy, the economy of *national sufficiency*.

THE RETURN TO EARTH

It is clear that it is necessary to decongest the cities and undertake the return to the land (*magna parens*), not to exploit it and then abandon it, but to live, live and to be perpetuated in its material and spiritual fertility. With this sense of the "subsistence economy," the land must be opened up to all families who have no reason to wander around in the anemic life of the city serving their vices.

In the land owned as a part of the family patrimony, men will feel their connection with their ancestors and will feel united with the real riches of the land, which will unite them with the Creator.

With its cosmic and divine virtues, the earth is called to solve not only the problem of a better distribution of temporal goods but also the problem of human life, so that man can serve his God.

The land which does not allow absolute mechanization, a mechanization possible in other sectors of the economy, has mysterious relationships with life itself: it is profoundly biological.

It is this biological sense, the sense of life, irreducible to any mechanical expression, that modern man must recover. If he does not recover this vital sense that he has lost, he will be able to rebuild a new economy, even a cooperative type, with hierarchical functioning, but it will be a mechanism of which man will feel himself a slave and not master. For this reason it is necessary for man to *live* a new economic order, and not to *build* it, as an external work.

It is the earth, fertile from man's work, that will make him live this order.

It is necessary to raise, then, the cry of return to the earth with a profoundly human sense. Only in this way will it be an economic and vital solution for modern man, who between papers and machines has lost his sense of reality.

To end this chapter, let us say that the imposition of an order in the problem of property and the production of the land requires a strong government, free from political compromises and liberal prejudices, which frees the country from the iron circle in which the international financiers and speculators have muzzled it and that dominates the petty interests of the capitalists and landowners; it must be a government that knows the whole of the reality of the country and the world, that is not intimidated by the popular clamor raised by the pack of politicians. It must be a government that, guided only by the common good, common to families according to their different status and social function (because there must be poor families and rich families), imposes the most advantageous arrangement.

Chapter 3

Industrial Production

IN THE FIRST CHAPTER we studied the concept of economy itself and we showed that because of its proximate formal object, that is, the procurement of the material goods useful to man, the economy seeks the improvement of man in his material aspect; hence, the economy is essentially a human or moral science.

It is a moral science, not because man concerns himself with it (he also concerns himself with chemistry and physics, and these are not moral sciences) nor because he constructs or builds it up (since he also builds works of art, and these are not moral in themselves), but rather because by its very nature the economy is ordered to the service of man. An economy that does not serve man, one that does not contribute to his human welfare, to the universal, common social welfare, and not just of one class, is not an economy. Hence, capitalism is not an economy; socialism is not an economy. Modern treatise writers and modern universities, who multiply economic theories, or, rather, formulas for increasing wealth, ignore economics. In all of these systems and studies, there will be a profitable waste of technology and of economic observations that could be healthily integrated into the economy; however, this integration has not been carried out. On the contrary, these economic elements have been incorporated into the anti-economic understanding of modern economy, which has resulted in a machine that devours human well-being. In a word: modern economics is anti-economic.

In the second chapter, we studied the phenomenon of the earth's production, and denounced the disorder of the modern economy, which by its essence desires the constant increase of profit, which tries to absorb production of land into industrial and commercial production. We affirmed that it was necessary for the production of the land to recover primacy of place in regulating all the production to which the economic reality itself destines it. Certain countries will be able to give greater impetus to industry, while others, due to their geographical conditions, will give it to agriculture and livestock. However, the economic rhythm of the world should not be dragged around by mercantilism or industrialism, and still, a particular country will not abandon its agriculture to dedicate itself exclusively to industry. This has been the great mistake "*contra naturam*" committed by England at the dawn of capitalism and definitively sanctioned in 1842 with the Corn Laws. It is an error whose deadly consequences are being felt now, when it finds itself without the agriculture that provides man's primary sustenance and without markets in which to place its outmoded industrial products.

We promote the return to an economic production that is rural as opposed to urban, domestic as opposed to mercantile; we endorse this as something necessary and even as imposed by the very rhythm of the world economic which is frankly protectionist.

INDUSTRIAL PRODUCTION

And what becomes of industrial production? Will it be necessary to discard the stupendous expansion of technology and machines as useless? In no way. It will only be necessary to assign it a secondary place, since it serves to satisfy man's needs that are also secondary. No one will find it difficult to admit this, if they consider that the only economy is that which perfects man, that which satisfies his material human well-being. Now, this well-being is hierarchical: because what comes first it is to eat, then to dress and live, and only then to enjoy the superfluous, which is what industry preferably supplies. Hence, production must also be hierarchical. The land must prevail over industry. In proposing this I am fully aware that it must seem blasphemous to those who believe in comfort and understand man's mission on earth according to the vision outlined by President Hoover, when he says: "The man who has a standard automobile, a standard radio, and an hour and a half less daily work, he has a fuller life and more personality than he had before."[a]

Another question is whether it will be possible to restore industry to its rightful secondary place.

Obviously, in man's current anemic state, it is absurd to imagine it. This is because, while industrial life has acquired a monstrous corpulence (remember the magnificent, victorious history of industrialism with the age of cotton, cast iron, the steam-powered machine, chemicals, electricity, the gas motor, inventions now used mathematically in the rationalization of industrial life), while industrial life, I say, has acquired a monstrous corpulence, man continuing in the gap opened by Luther, Descartes, and Rousseau,[1,b] has been losing his

1 See J. Maritain, *The Three Reformers*, and Nikolai Berdiaeff [sometimes spelt Berdyaev] *The New Middle Ages.*

a Meinvielle gives no citation for this text. Other sources cite the text as: "The man who has a standard automobile, a standard telephone, a standard bathtub, a standard electric light, a standard radio, and one and one-half hours less average daily labor is more of a man and has a fuller life and more individuality than he has without them." Cited in Lee Vinsel, *Moving Violations: Automobiles, Experts, and Regulations in the United States* (Baltimore: Johns Hopkins University Press, 2019), 58.

b Jacques Maritain, *Three Reformers: Luther, Descartes, Rousseau* (London:

personality, and today he is a simple grain of dust, driven by infinite circumstances. He has lost his dominating power, in such a way that while the beast has been increasing in size and courage, the tamer has lost his control.

It is not difficult to envision what the fate of the tamer must be, weakened in the face of the enraged beast.

He is doubtless a poetic figure. However, it is quite possible that men cannot agree on how to limit the power of the machine. In the meantime, it kills them.

In short: the problem of production has no solution until the more general problem of the economy itself is solved, and this in turn, until the problem of life is solved, as I explained in the first chapter. It is a trivial observation that specialists must keep in mind, who attempt to impose a local order without paying attention to the total order. Synthesis is prior to analysis, the one to the many.

MORAL JUSTIFICATION OF CAPITAL

After these preliminary considerations, let us study the organization that must exist within industrial life itself.

We will have to justify capital, salary, management, and machinery, and also harmonize their rights. Note that I justify these elements in general, in the abstract, indicating the essential structure that they can and should have. I am not justifying these elements as they have been established in capitalism, precisely because capitalism has already given a perverse and unfair conformation to these elements that are good in themselves.

This justification must be done from the moral point of view, that is, from the point of view of human action as human. Can these elements be justified as human acts and, if so, to what extent? Can they be acts of virtue, or are they instead intrinsically vicious acts?

Sheen & Ward, 1928). Nikolai Berdyaev, "The New Middle Ages," in *The End of Our Time*, trans. Donald Attwater (New York: Sheed & Ward, 1933), 67–120.

If the first, they can be justified as long as they truly proceed with right order; if the second, they are never justified. If the first, as long as they are good they will also be beneficial; if the second, they will be disastrous.

Now, with these assumptions in place, let's see if capital is justified.

Capital is justified as the exercise of a virtue that Saint Thomas calls magnificence. If we remember correctly, in a previous chapter we said that private property has a social function, a common destination: common use, as Saint Thomas says. By virtue of this common destination of external goods, Saint Thomas says:

> Whatever certain people have in superabundance is due, by natural law, to the purpose of succoring the poor. For this reason Ambrose says, and his words are embodied in the *Decretals* (Dist. xlvii, can. Sicut ii): *It is the hungry man's bread that you withhold, the naked man's cloak that you store away, the money that you bury in the earth is the price of the poor man's ransom and freedom.*[2]

Is it necessary, then, to get rid of what is superfluous, that is, of what is left over once the need and decorum of one's own condition have been satisfied, and donate it to the poor in the form of alms? This is not exactly the case. This money can be invested in companies that provide work and bread to the needy.

This is the doctrine that Pope Pius XI admirably taught in his encyclical on *Reconstruction of the Social Order*, when he writes:

> Expending larger incomes so that opportunity for gainful work may be abundant, provided,

2 ST II-II, q. 66, a. 7.

> however, that this work is applied to producing really useful goods, ought to be considered, as We deduce from the principles of the Angelic Doctor [cf. ST II-II, q. 134], an outstanding exemplification of the virtue of munificence and one particularly suited to the needs of the times.[c]

The virtue of magnificence, as Aquinas explains, orders the right use of large amounts of money, just as liberality commands the use of money in general, even if it is little. Hence, the person who accumulates superfluous money and removes it from common use would be guilty of the sin of avarice.

Hence, it follows that the economic concept of capital is justified by the exercise of the Christian virtue of magnificence.

What, in fact, is capital? It is accumulated wealth that is invested in a company for the production of other wealth, and thus the community benefits, and this in such a way that capital, as such, first seeks to benefit the community, the poor, because it is the investment of *whatever certain people have in superabundance* [that] *is due, by natural law, to the purpose of succoring the poor.*[d]

I do not think it is necessary to show that this is not the understanding that capitalism has forged of capital. Reserving a deeper critique of the capitalist understanding of capital for the next chapter, let it suffice for now to say that for capitalism, capital is money that produces more money, that forms concentrated money. This is exactly the opposite of true capital since, far from making capital a medium that spreads the benefit of money to the community, it makes it a magnet that accumulates money quickly and absorbingly in the hands of the lucky individual who possesses it. That is why, while the

---

c Pius XI, "Quadragesimo Anno," 51.

d ST II-II, q. 66, a. 7.

capitalist accumulates and grows rich in a fantastic way, the multitude is continuously dispossessed, until it ends up in true misery and unemployment.

The eminently social, common destination of the wealth invested in capital has been forgotten. Furthermore, it has been forgotten that capital is inherently sterile when it is not employed for the work of intellect or the muscles. Who or what makes the new material riches? Man's work: the entrepreneur's initiative, who, with his intellect and tenacious will, will uncover the most efficient and fastest way for a better production of wealth; the laborers' work, which, applied under the direction of the entrepreneur's intelligence, will produce wealth. The production of wealth is an *effect proper to work itself*. The capital invested in means of production (machines, equipment) is an *instrument*, a necessary one if you want, but a simple instrument whose fruition comes from work. Hence, labor is superior to capital as the principal cause is superior to the instrumental cause. For example, in the making of a book, the author's rights are first and superior to the rights of ink and pen. It is true that capital has rights, but its rights come after the rights of labor.

As Jacques Maritain writes:

> In theory and in the abstract, a system of association between money and productive labor may easily be conceived in which the money invested in an undertaking represented an owner's share in the means of production, and was used to feed the undertaking, enabling it to procure the needful material, equipment and resources in such a way that, the undertaking being productive and producing profits, a share in

> such profits should be returned to the capital.[3,e]

In other words, capital should feed work, and not work capital. This is exactly the same thing that St. Thomas teaches, when he writes: "He that entrusts his money to a merchant or craftsman so as to form *a kind of society*, does not transfer the ownership of his money to them, for it remains his, so that at his risk the merchant speculates with it, or the craftsman uses it for his craft, and consequently he may lawfully demand as something belonging to him, part of the profits derived from his money."[4,f]

From this it follows, against the doctrine of Marx, that capital is entitled to a share of the profit, and that profit, in itself, is not an usurpation of the worker's labor as the simplistic theory of surplus value claimed.

It also follows, against the blatant injustice of liberal capitalism, that the rights of capital are subsequent to the rights of labor. Capitalism has inverted the rights of labor and those of capital, suffocating the former under the greedy clutches of the latter. As Jacques Maritain writes:

> Instead of being considered as a mere feeder enabling a living organism, which the productive undertaking is, to procure the necessary material, equipment and replenishing, money has come to be considered *the living organism*, and the undertaking with its human activities as the feeder and instrument of money; so that the profits cease to be the normal fruit of the undertaking fed with money, and become the

3 Maritain, *Religion et culture*, 97.
4 ST II-II, q. 78, a. 2.

e Trans. from Maritain, "Religion and Culture," 56.
f The citation should be ST II-II, q. 78, a. 2, ad 5.

> normal fruit of the money fed by the undertaking. . . . the immediate consequence is to give the rights of dividend precedence over those of salary.[5,g]

It is necessary to cry out against this injustice that constitutes the very core of capitalism, an injustice that goes unnoticed even by the workers themselves, who consider it as a most natural and just thing. Capital is an instrument of labor. Labor must use capital. For this reason, the primary and only desire that moves the capitalist, namely, to ensure profit and increase capital, is unjust. This is secondary, and comes after human well-being has been sufficiently ensured, according to the condition of each one, of all the executors and operators who have put their activity in the company. In addition, as I said before, and this follows from the doctrine of the Church taught by Saint Thomas, the capitalist who invests his money must not seek first of all his profit, his benefit, his gain, but must first try to provide work and with it the human well-being of those less fortunate than himself in the possession of wealth; only once this primary requirement of capital has been satisfied, can he benefit himself from the resulting profits.

For many, this reasoning will seem to be unfounded; it will seem like a fantasy. I know well that capitalism and the capitalist move only for profit, for the thirst for gold, by the desire to accumulate. This is why in the first chapter I affirmed that capitalism is unfair, nefarious, and is kneaded in the sin of greed. For this reason, I am affirming that capitalism has risen and rises with the theft of the worker's inalienable rights. Hence, what Saint John Chrysostom affirmed of great fortunes

5 Maritain, *Religion et culture*, 97.

g Trans. from Maritain, "Religion and Culture," 57.

applies most justly to capitalism: "At the origin of all the great fortunes there is injustice, violence, or theft."

However, despite knowing that it is a childish insistence to teach that the rights of capital must be demanded after the sufficient rights of labor, I reaffirm it. I do so, first, because the truth must be expressed; secondly, because this teaching is more necessary than ever; thirdly, because from the first line of this book I have announced that I would only formulate a judgment of value, an axiological judgment, regarding the modern economic reality. This will disappoint those who would like a practical formula that, without abandoning capitalism, would fix the troubled economy. However, the truth is that the only truly practical solution is to abandon the essentially unjust capitalism.

BUSINESS

As we said, work is first and capital is secondary. The two are associated in a business. Nevertheless, there is the work of the employer and the work of the worker. The first is the work of the intellect and will: the entrepreneur takes a risk.

What counterweight will balance the entrepreneur's risks? Capital also takes risks. What counterweight will balance it?

On the contrary, the laborer does not risk anything. In his condition as a man without private income, a condition which that does not allow him to wait for the income of the company so as to live on these profits, he must work for a daily wage that ensures his and his family's subsistence, as we will explain shortly when we speak of salary. Hence, strictly speaking, the worker is not entitled to a share in the profits.

Thus, properly speaking, the salaried worker is not part of the business. Although this is for reasons of a different nature, as Pius XI teaches in *Quadragesimo Anno*:

> We consider it more advisable, however, in the present condition of human society that, so far as

> is possible, the work-contract be somewhat modified by a partnership-contract, as is already being done in various ways and with no small advantage to workers and owners. Workers and other employees thus become sharers in ownership or management or participate in some fashion in the profits received.

Given this, there are now several questions to ask. 1) Does business—association of work and capital—need to make a profit? 2) Can this profit be the business' "first mover"? 3) How should this profit be distributed?

Three extremely difficult points, which must be carefully examined, from the point of view of the moral law.

THE BUSINESS' PROFIT

Does business—association of work and capital—need to make a profit?

I answer yes, because both capital and labor risk their own resources, and such a risk must have a just reward. If there were no prospect of profit, who would expose their resources? Who would venture into businesses?

The risk justifies profit, as the scholastics have seen; they consider the benefits derived from money invested in a company as something just, as they considered interest on borrowed money as unjust.[6]

In order to appreciate and understand the importance of this reason, we are going to fully transcribe the difficulty that Saint Thomas sets up when he asks if it is lawful to demand some profit for borrowed money

The saint proposes this difficulty:

> The lender, by transferring his ownership of a sum of money removes the money further from

6 ST II-II, q. 78, a. 2.

> himself than he who entrusts it to a merchant or craftsman. Now it is lawful to receive interest for money entrusted to a merchant or craftsman. Therefore it is also lawful to receive interest for money lent.[7,h]

Aquinas replies to this objection by saying:

> He who lends money transfers the ownership of the money to the borrower. Hence the borrower holds the money at his own risk and is bound to pay it all back: wherefore the lender must not exact more. On the other hand he that entrusts his money to a merchant or craftsman so as to form a kind of society, does not transfer the ownership of his money to them, for it remains his, so that at his risk the merchant speculates with it, or the craftsman uses it for his craft, and consequently he may lawfully demand as something belonging to him, part of the profits derived from his money.

The risk involved is therefore compensated by the fair gain. However, can this gain be the company's "first mover," that is, the primary incentive for its operations?

To ask this question is to ask the same question to which St. Thomas gives a solution in the *Summa*, when he asks "whether, in trading, it is lawful to sell a thing at a higher price than what was paid for it?"[8] Aquinas answers by saying that trading or commerce for profit:

7 ST II-II, q. 78, a. 2

8 ST II-II, q. 77, a. 4.

h The complete citation should be ST II-II, q. 78, a. 2, obj. 5 and ad 5.

> is justly deserving of blame, because, considered in itself, it satisfies the greed for gain, which knows no limit and tends to infinity. Hence trading, considered in itself, has a certain debasement attaching thereto, insofar as, by its very nature, it does not imply a virtuous or necessary end. Nevertheless gain which is the end of trading, though not implying, by its nature, anything virtuous or necessary, does not, in itself, connote anything sinful or contrary to virtue: wherefore nothing prevents gain from being directed to some necessary or even virtuous end, and thus trading becomes lawful. Thus, for instance, a man may intend the moderate gain which he seeks to acquire by trading for the upkeep of his household, or for the assistance of the needy: or again, a man may take to trade for some public advantage, for instance, lest his country lack the necessaries of life, and seek gain, not as an end, but as payment for his labor.

It is clear from this admirable doctrine of the Angelic Doctor that "profit cannot be the motive for a capitalist enterprise." There should be some profit because capital is risked, but profit cannot be sought simply for profit's sake. There must be "honest movers" (that is, good motives) that justify the investment of money in a business, such as, for example, benefiting the community with a new useful production, giving work to the indigent, or even a suitable support for investors and their families.

How many practical applications could be made of this doctrine, which is the Catholic doctrine of economics! Were a resourceful Catholic investor to proceed in the light of these principles, what useful works would he bring about in favor of his fellow men, raising the economic status of the indigent classes and, with it, raising their cultural and religious situation! Indeed, in this case capital would recover its proper role of *disseminating goods in the community,* and not, on the other hand, as now happens in this profit economy, which *takes up the goods of the community in order to accumulate them in the hands of a minority* that exclusively enjoys them!

How should the profit of a business be distributed?

Speaking in accord with strict law of commutative justice, once all the obligations with operators and consumers have been satisfied, the profit that comes from a business belongs to the business owner (or owners) who managed the business and to the investors who made this management possible. Commenting on the famous article by Aquinas, Cardinal Cajetan explains the principles of this distribution so that justice is carried out.[9] Cajetan comments that the benefits must be proportional to the risks to which each partner is exposed according to the amount of capital that they invest or the work and initiative that they contribute to make this capital productive.

Nevertheless, although according to commutative justice there is no further obligation, for the Catholic there are other virtues besides commutative justice, and the Catholic must act in accord with them.

Earlier we said that the economic understanding of capital is justified by the exercise of the Christian virtue of magnificence. Capital is accumulated wealth that is invested in a business to produce other wealth and thus benefit the community. Hence it is necessary for the business to be regulated in such a way that the benefit is truly common, that is, for the community: accordingly, there is a need to set a limit to the profit of the shareholders and the entrepreneur. Likewise, the workers must be made to share in the profits. It is also necessary for the business to consider the interests of

9 ST II-II, q. 78, a. 2, ad 5.

consumers in order to produce truly useful articles. Lastly, it is essential that the company's profits are not made at the cost of ruinous competition with other entrepreneurs. Hence, the company must be organized in the real collaboration of capital, work, and management, and once organized in this way it must be harmonized within the framework of the profession and of the whole of economic life.

In other words, in the corporate regime, as I will explain when speaking of the *social economic order*, the company will achieve the regulation that makes it of collective benefit.

SALARY

Once the principles of a capitalist company in the Catholic understanding have been established, let us begin to explain salary. First of all, against the criticism of the socialists, let it be said that the rule of salary is necessary for workers. This is because the worker lives from his daily work: hence, he needs a daily payment. He cannot work in a business awaiting an uncertain benefit. Each day he needs the resources that ensure his own subsistence and that of his family: the daily wage is justified by the worker's indigent condition itself.

Note, however, that justifying the existence of salary or wages does not prevent us from strongly condemning the behavior of the capitalist in the remuneration of wages.

Such as with all the capitalists' efforts or, rather, the administrators of capital (who tend in turn to brazenly exploit the true capitalists), they seek their own profits, their own benefit, at all costs; as a consequence, they try to remunerate the workforce as little as possible, paying starvation wages, as was common in the 19th century, or else eliminate the work of the laborer all together by replacing it with that of women, children, or machines.

THE JUSTIFICATION OF WAGES

Two abuses regarding wages deserve careful consideration. First, we must remember that the worker's right to a fair salary is one of the most sacred rights. See how the Apostle James speaks:[10]

> Come now, you rich, weep and wail over your impending miseries. Your wealth has rotted away, your clothes have become moth-eaten, your gold and silver have corroded, and that corrosion will be a testimony against you; it will devour your flesh like a fire. You have stored up treasure for the last days. Behold, the wages you withheld from the workers who harvested your fields are crying aloud, and the cries of the harvesters have reached the ears of the Lord of hosts. You have lived on earth in luxury and pleasure; you have fattened your hearts for the day of slaughter. You have condemned; you have murdered the righteous one; he offers you no resistance.

This is the way that the Apostles spoke when condemning the exploitation of the poor. No one should be surprised, then, to hear harsh words of condemnation for the capitalist monster who has gotten drunk and gets drunk on the day laborer's sweat.

What is meant by "a just salary due to the worker," or, worded even better: what is the minimum salary whose limit cannot be lowered in any case without committing a flagrant injustice?

Leo XIII and Pius XI have answered the question in such a complete way that nothing new can be stated about it.

Work—especially that of the laborer and the employee—is the exercise of one's own activity geared towards the

10 Jas 5:1-6.

acquisition of those things necessary for the various uses of life, and mainly for self-preservation.

The man who makes use of his work lives from his work: he has the right to a human existence. Indeed, I go further: he has the right to a human and Christian existence. He cannot be used as a machine or as a commodity or as a workhorse or just as a fancy animal. Therefore, if he works, that is: if he uses his strengths in another man's business, then the worker has the right to be provided by that other man with the necessary resources for a human life, worthy of man.

A human life: therefore, at least what is necessary for the sustenance of a frugal worker with good morals (Leo XIII) and that of his family (Pius XI). Since his is a human life, it is: typical of man, meaning, to live himself and to live as a family with his wife and his children. The absolute family wage is due to every worker. The head of the family is one thing, one being with his wife and his children. It is up to him to sustain them. When his wife and children are hungry, it is the father who suffers and feels the hunger. Hence Pope Pius XI says:

> To abuse the years of childhood and the limited strength of women is grossly wrong. . . . It is an intolerable abuse, and to be abolished at all cost, for mothers on account of the father's low wage to be forced to engage in gainful occupations outside the home [the same could be said of children who must engage in street selling and other similar labors] to the neglect of their proper cares and duties, especially the training of children.[i]

Note that the family wage is owed to every worker as a minimum wage, even if he is single, because it is the human wage, which is owed to him as a man. If he doesn't get

i Meinvielle gives no citation, but the text is from Pius XI, "Quadragesimo Anno," 71.

married, that is a matter that concerns only him. The employer owes him the human wage which is, at the very least, the family wage.

A human life: however, a life that has only what is strictly necessary for each day's sustenance, in which nothing can be saved in anticipation of tomorrow, is not a human life. For this reason, the just salary demands something more than what is strictly necessary for the daily sustenance of the family. Hence, Pius XI says that "We have shown above how much it helps the common good for workers and other employees, by setting aside some part of their income which remains after necessary expenditures, to attain gradually to the possession of a moderate amount of wealth."[j]

The just minimum wage also includes a humane and Christian treatment.

A humane treatment: "With respect to daily work, therefore, care ought to be taken not to extend it beyond the hours that human strength warrants. The length of rest intervals ought to be decided on the basis of the varying nature of the work, of the circumstances of time and place, and of the physical condition of the workers themselves" (Leo XIII).[k]

A humane treatment: by this I understand that the division of labor imposed by "Taylorization" must be rejected.[l] It is not

j Again, Meinvielle gives no citation, but the text is from Pius XI, "Quadragesimo Anno," 74.

k Meinvielle gives no citation, but the text is from Leo XIII, "Rerum Novarum" (Encyclical, Rome, May 15, 1891), 59.

l "Taylorization: System of scientific management advocated by Fred W. Taylor. In Taylor's view, the task of factory management was to determine the best way for the worker to do the job, to provide the proper tools and training, and to provide incentives for good performance. He broke each job down into its individual motions, analyzed these to determine which were essential, and timed the workers with a stopwatch. With unnecessary motion eliminated, the worker, following a machinelike routine, became far more productive." *Taylorism*, in *Encyclopaedia Briannica*, by The Editors of Encyclopaedia Britannica.

permissible for man to submit to the mechanical, automatic repetition of the same gesture, without any of his own initiative. Man is not an ox man, contrary to what Taylor imagined and said. He has a right to human nobility.[m]

A treatment which, in addition to being humane, *must also be Christian*: this is because the worker has been ransomed by Christ, and is loved by Christ in a special way, since He too was a worker. As a result, the laborer has the right to be considered as a Christian and opportunities to fulfill his religious duties and sanctify the Lord's day must be facilitated.

As explained above, the minimum salary can never be denied, not for any reason and in no case, even if civil legislation authorizes denying it. "If through necessity or fear of a worse evil," writes Leo XIII, "the workman accepts harder conditions because an employer or contractor will afford him no better, he is made the victim of force and injustice."[n] With unemployment, now there is no shortage of those who exploit the low demand for labor to unfairly remunerate the laborer's work. This is a pernicious abuse: if a company does not have the resources to pay a just salary, it cannot demand an ordinary job from the worker either. The only thing that can be demanded is the work that is paid for. If wages decrease below what is fair, the amount of work must decrease in the same proportion.

Thus far we have tried to quickly determine the minimum wage, whose limit cannot be lowered without a disastrous

m The reference to "ox man" would seem to refer to this citation of Taylor: "One of the very first requirements for a man who is fit to handle pig iron as a regular occupation is that he shall be so stupid and so phlegmatic that he more nearly resembles in his mental make-up the ox than any other type. The man who is mentally alert and intelligent is for this very reason entirely unsuited to what would, for him, be the grinding monotony of work of this character" (Frederick Winslow Taylor, *The Principles of Scientific Management* (New York, Harper & Brothers, 1919), 59.)

n Again, Meinvielle gives no citation, but the text is from Leo XIII, "Rerum Novarum," 45.

violation of strict justice.

Will an entrepreneur be content with this? Not at all. As the *Code* of the International Union of Social Studies of Mechelen says: "The minimum wage does not fulfill the demands of the justice. Various principal causes entail, whether for justice or equity, an increase above the minimum. Thus, for example, a more abundant production or the greater or lesser prosperity of the company, require an increase in wages. In addition, there must be a hierarchy in salaries, according to the economic function that is performed. It is not just that the work of the stonemason is paid equally to that of the electrician."[o]

This is a commonsense truth, but a truth against which capitalism conspires. Thus, for instance, it is said that the doorman of the Ritz Hotel in Paris earns 300,000 francs a year, while a professor at the College de France earns 45,000 francs. It is more remunerative to serve the pleasures or vices of a plutocracy than to supply it with intellectual elements.[11]

To finish this question about wages, which we had to explain in a hurry, without saying anything about the *Allocations familiers* [child benefits] to help large families and insurance against accidents at work, etc., let us say that although the wage system is fair in itself, it is urgent that

11 Malcor, "L'économie contemporaine : travail, assurances, capitalisme."

o See Union Internationale d'Etudes Sociales, *Code Social: Esquisse d'une synthese sociale catholique* (Montreal: Éditions de L'École Sociale Populaire, 1944), 77: "Le second point à considérer est celui de la situation de l'entreprise. Il serait injuste d'exiger d'elle des salaires exagérés qu'elle ne saurait supporter sans courir à la ruine. D'autre part le salaire minimum n'épuise pas toujours les exigences de la justice. Au-dessus du minimum, diverses causes principales entraînent, soit en justice, soit en équité, une majoration: a) Une production plus abondante, plus parfaite ou plus économe que la normale; b) La prospérité plus ou moins grande de l'entreprise à laquelle l'ouvrier est attaché."

today it be tempered by the rule of society. Whether in part because of capitalist exploitation, or because of the outcries of the workers' exploiters, the truth is that the worker and the employee have an instinctive aversion to salaried work. Hence, we must say with Pius XI that, "We consider it more advisable, however, in the present condition of human society that, so far as is possible, the work-contract be somewhat modified by a partnership-contract, as is already being done in various ways and with no small advantage to workers and owners. Workers and other employees thus become sharers in ownership or management or participate in some fashion in the profits received."[p]

MACHINERY

However, the entire doctrine of fair wages is perfectly useless today, because capitalism provides more expeditious resources to circumvent it.

The work of the laborer is replaced by that of women and children, who are paid less, and above all by the work of the machine.

It is something monstrous that it is easier for a little girl to be placed in a plant than for a worker, father of a family. Here is the height of capitalist exploitation. However, what is beyond all description is that the entire endeavor of the capitalist is to establish the form of an automatic movement of his factory that eliminates labor in order to increase his individual profit.

In effect, it is well-known that the desire of the capitalist to super-multiply profits is realized by delivering a product to the market that is less expensive than the current one. For this he will apply a new technical procedure that increases the machine's work and reduces labor. That is to say: his whole effort is to dislodge the worker by means of the machine. One

p Meinvielle gives no citation, but the text is from Pius XI, "Quadragesimo Anno," 65.

example among a thousand: at one point the manufacturer Harrison in the United States produced 50 radiators a day, costing 10 man-hours.[q] Thanks to a more sophisticated instrument, in 1929 he managed to produce 10,000 radiators in 40 minutes of work. He saved 93 percent on labor. It is not about condemning the industrialist Harrison. If this gentleman had not applied this procedure he would have perished in the industrial competition. It is about showing in an example the cruelty of an economic system feverish by the acceleration of profit, to the detriment of the majority of humanity.

Capitalism abuses machines in two ways. First, because capitalism monopolizes its undeniable beneficial strength to the detriment of the community. Like all goods, machines have a common, social purpose: it is therefore just that they benefit the worker as well as capital, and the worker before capital, because, as we said before, the rights of labor are higher than the rights of capital, since without work capital is a sterile good.

This is the first abuse that capital makes of the machine.

Related to this first abuse is the second, namely, that not only does the worker not share the benefit of machines, but capitalism rather uses this benefit as a means to dislodge the worker, to kill the worker.

Some will say that these are the requirements of technology, of progress.

But, I ask: would it be licit to feed machines with human flesh, under the pretext that it is a better fuel than coal? Is it licit, then, to submerge more than twenty million men in absolute misery, not counting their families, to place others in true misery because of the starving wages that they are paid,

q Presumably Herbert Champion Harrison (October 4, 1876 – March 6, 1927), founder of the Harrison Radiator Company in 1910 which was later sold to United Motors Company, and then, along with them, to General Motors.

and thereby create immense world despair, and all because it is necessary to respect the infinite acceleration of the machine?

The question is: is the machine made for man, or man for the machine?

I think that no one doubts that the superpower of machines is one of the causes, although not the main one, of the current economic malaise.

Remember that today, thanks to mass production imposed by Hoover and Ford, the United States has a production capacity that exceeds the consumption of the entire world in some items.

Thus, for example: "The production capacity of the American automobile industry is 8,000,000 cars, while world consumption in 1929 barely exceeded 600,000.

The American shoe industry can produce 900 million shoes annually, while American consumption does not exceed 300 million shoes.

The coal mines are equipped to produce 750,000,000 tons of coal, when the American market cannot absorb 500,000,000."[12] In the oil, coal, steel, wool, and silk industries, technical instruments are available that represent a production capacity three times the volume of sales.

At the same time, all countries are eager to develop their industries. Even India has raised its industry, equal to that of Europe, and has closed its markets to the old English industries. In a few years, Russia intends to bring about a production more powerful than the American one.

The dizzying delirium of profit, capriciously accelerating the potentiality of machines, threatens to wolf down the entire human race after having exploited the proletarian mass for 150 years.

Will man know how to stop the runaway speed in time? At the beginning I said that in the face of the machine, that has

12 Pierre Lucius, *Faillite du capitalisme? ... Une explication de la crise mondiale* (Impr. J. Dumoulin, 1932), 103.

been increasing its corpulence and rage, modern man is simply a grain of dust, driven by infinite circumstances. His fate is not difficult to predict.

BOURGEOISIE AND PROLETARIAT

We have examined industrial production, to arrive at the conclusion that everything is established in such a way in the capitalist economy that the bourgeois is omnipotent and tyrannical in front of the poor, in front of the day laborer in particular, and that the bourgeois uses this omnipotence to squeeze the last drop of dignity out of him.

This is not simply literary expression. Ordinary dealings with workers has shown me first-hand the vileness with which they are treated. Their dignity as a Christian has been ripped from them: the worker, loved with predilection by Christ who wanted to be poor and to be a worker, today has a concentrated, hopeless hatred against Christ, against his Church and the ministers of the Crucified. (Living with them, this is easily verified.) Who has deposited that hatred in their hearts? The bourgeois, the capitalist, the Catholic bourgeois. This is because if newspapers, if books, if cinema and theater poison the worker, the fault lies with the bourgeois, who, with the desire to get rich, ingested the poison. If secular schools and atheistic universities poison with their childish ignorance, the fault lies with the bourgeois.

The worker's dignity as a man has been stripped from him: since the bourgeois who, in the end, is nothing but a worker with more luck, has considered him as a despised commodity, which is used as long as he serves. It is true that he is provided with comforts, bourgeois superfluities (sports, cinema, reading), but at the cost of his human dignity, which has been violated by the machine.

But today the worker is desperate and in the face of dropsical capitalism he feels strong. He no longer accepts "to serve:" he wants to be the master.

The pace of events suggests that the time has come for his empire. From the French Revolution up to now, the bourgeoisie has dominated, just as the aristocracy had previously dominated, and before them, the priestly power. Today, with the bourgeoisie exhausted, the scepter will pass to the proletariat.

For this reason—writes Berdiaeff—just as before it was necessary to teach the bourgeois to respect the human dignity of the working classes, so today the workers must be taught that "the bourgeois and the gentlemen also are human beings, that they must be treated accordingly and their dignity and worth respected. This, at least, is the position in Soviet Russia, and the same will probably come about one day in the West."[13,r]

Then, as now, it will be necessary to preach "*oportune et importune*" [in season and out of season] that man of any social condition bears in his being the image of God, has been rescued by Christ, and is called to eternal life. "In the face of this divine dignity, all class differences, all political passions, all the superimpositions that daily social intercourse has accumulated on the human soul, are insignificant and vain."[s] The Church of Jesus Christ, which is the same Christ prolonged and made visible among us, then, as now, will remember that "it is useless for a man to gain the whole world if he loses his soul."[t]

And that the supreme well-being of man in heaven and on earth is in the love of all, united in the One who has put His wealth in giving His life for us.

---

13 Nicolas Berdiaeff, *Le christianisme et la Lutte des classes*, trans. I. P. and H. M. (Editions du Dromadaire, 1932), 195.

---

r Eng. trans. from Nicholas Berdyaev, *Christianity and Class War*, trans. Donald Attwater (London: Sheed & Ward, 1934), 122.

s This text is in quotes in the original Spanish, but without any reference.

t Cf. Mk 8:36; Mt 16:26.

Chapter 4

Finances

When outlining the nature of capitalism in the first chapter, we discovered its fundamental law that can be summarized in its definition: "the increase of profit due to the increase of production and consumption." Profit, infinite and insatiable, governs the entire orientation of the modern economic system, so that things are consumed in order to produce and what is produced is to make a profit. Production regulates consumption and finances govern production. We showed how an economy governed by this capital vice would be a disastrous economy for man and itself, because it would carry its own ruin in its entrails without ever being able, not even for an instant, to provide the economic well-being of man.

In the two previous chapters we examined the ordering of production, both agricultural and industrial, and justified the concepts of property, labor, and capital. However, in the explanation of these concepts, we continually made the effort to point out the uselessness of that whole ordering if the finances that govern the economic life today, with their violent shocks, are not properly functioning.

Hence, in this fourth chapter we undertake the study of

finances. This, then, is the key to these pages, at least as an explanation and critique of capitalism. The study of finances will reveal to us the fundamental point that sustains the entire modern economy called capitalism; this will reveal to us the root of the present economic crisis, a definitive, insoluble crisis. Some relief can be given, but this will be as an improvement that heralds the fatal outcome of the dying.

However, since it is not our primary intent to criticize capitalism, but rather to propose the Catholic understanding of the economy, in the course of this chapter we will try to make a clear Catholic notion of money, capital, and credit appear.

TRUE RICHES

Now then, true riches are what Saint Thomas calls natural riches, that is, the products of the land and industry, because only they can remedy indigence and provide the sufficiency of goods to live virtuously.[1] For this reason, the head of the household and the prudent politician acquire and store up these riches that are so useful for the domestic and political community, because without what is necessary for life, governance of the house or of the city is not possible.[2]

However, the acquisition of these goods presupposes their production. Once produced, they need to circulate so that those produced by us reach others and they can take advantage of them, while those produced by them can be taken advantage of by us. It is therefore necessary to exchange natural wealth.

Clearly in the first domestic community, this exchange was not necessary; since everything was produced at home and everything belonged to the head of the family, who

1 ST II-II, q. 118, a. 2.

2 Commentary of Saint Thomas to the *Politics* of Aristotle, Bk. 1, lecture 2.

distributed the work as well as its products. However, as towns and cities were formed, an elementary division of labor appeared, and the exchange of natural wealth, known as barter, became imperative.[3]

From this first natural exchange (the model of all equitable exchange, because I give so much of this that is worth as much for this other that is worth the same), artificial exchange or, exchange by means of money, was born. Since relations between men were expanding and extending even to distant lands, it was not easy to trade natural riches such as wine, wheat, and the like. For this reason, in order to carry out these exchanges in distant places, it was established that something should be given and received that, in addition to its value, would be easy to carry, for example, metals such as copper, iron, and silver. At first, the metal was determined by its weight or quantity only: but later, to avoid the work of measuring and weighing, a stamp was printed on the metal as a guarantee of a certain quantity.[4]

MONEY

Money is nothing more than what is adopted as an instrument of exchange. In itself, as money, it does not have any mysterious current or magnetic force. Its value is pure change: it will be, therefore, greater or less the greater or lesser the number of things that can be acquired with its unit. Hence, it is made to circulate, because only in this way does it fulfill its essential function as an instrument for exchanging natural wealth, that is, the products of the land and of industry.

Delving deeper into this notion, let us note that it is not necessary for money *qua* money to be a good or merchandise, or something that has an intrinsic value. In its primitive

3 Commentary of Saint Thomas to the *Politics* of Aristotle, Bk. 1, lecture 7.

4 Commentary of Saint Thomas to the *Politics* of Aristotle, Bk. 1, lecture 7.

meaning, money was a bond of things of value, indeed, a bond equivalent to their value. Hence, we have different forms of money: ingot-money, leather-money, bean-money, cattle-money, salt-money, shell-money. Whatever was to be used as money needed to meet three conditions: of course, it must first be recognized everywhere as a pledge to give and receive; next, it must preserve the recognized value in a lasting and immutable way; and, lastly, it should not fix the value of all other goods, but rather ensure that the relation of their reciprocal value is not disturbed, and that it (that is, the money) is only understood as representative of the expression of these relations of values.

With the introduction of money, two great changes took place in commercial relations. First of all, exchange became a purchase; in other words, the pure real relationship turned into a personal relationship, the real contract into a consensual contract. Second, price replaced commodity. It is the same as the piece of personal property, the object of purchase or of exchange. The price is the estimate or the comparison of the merchandise with what is not directly merchandise, but only an equivalent or representation of the merchandise and intermediary between goods.

With the introduction of money, merchandise, corresponding transactions, and needs were no longer directly compared with each other, but rather considered only mediately in relation to each other, referring their value to money, the generally adopted measure of price.

Money as such, that is, in its quality as money, can therefore never be a commodity. If someone considers money as merchandise, either as a simple thing of value because of the material of which it is composed, then it is no longer currency. If someone considers money as merchandise because of other comforts or advantages that are added to it and whose use can be separated from it or at least be appreciated separately (because they are not essentially linked with it) as means of commercial relations, then it is no longer currency.[5] Money could have value, not *qua* money, but in light of the material that it is made up of. In this case, it is necessary to ensure that its nominal value coincides with this value of the thing, in order to prevent it from being traded for it as if it were a commodity.[6]

Now, if money is not a real, independent good, neither can it have a real independent value of its own; it is nothing more than a sign of value that can be used to redeem other real values, but only insofar as there are other values that can be mutually exchanged.

MONEY TRADING

In short, money only has a purely nominal value, representative of natural wealth. It is not meant to be traded.

However, Aristotle observes that as soon as money was introduced, there were those who traded money itself for profit. These were the money changers or bankers, with their art called "*nummularia*." Aristotle, and after him St. Thomas and the scholastics, call this the *artificial pecuniary* art, whose proper task is the artificial production of profit by money trading. He states that this art based on enrichment by exchanging money is blameworthy, just as the understanding of many who imagine that only money is wealth is blameworthy and foolish.

To believe that only money is wealth—continues Aristotle—is an absurdity, because the value of true wealth cannot depend on the will of men; however, the dignity and usefulness of money depend on the will of the same social community, which can, when it pleases, annul its value and replace it with another: hence, it follows that money is not

5 ST II-II, q. 78, a. 1 ad 6.

6 See Alberto Weiss O.P, *Apologia del Cristianismo*, vol. 8 (Barcelona: Juan Gili, 1906).

true wealth. In addition, that one can have abundant money and perish from hunger, as the fable tells of Midas, who, with an insatiable desire for money, asked the gods that everything he touched should turn to gold, a "gift" that was granted. As a result, he starved to death, because all the food that was presented to him turned into gold.

All of this shows—and it is fitting to remind the modern economy of this, because it has lost the basic understanding of money—that finances or *pecuniary art* does not have an end in itself, as if it were the supreme thing to which a person should aspire. The true wealth of a country is not computed by the gold it has stored in its coffers. The United States, despite its enormous gold reserves, is a country with a miserable economy because it fails to provide human well-being to its millions of unemployed.

However, as Aristotle and Saint Thomas accurately demonstrate, there is a perverse instinct in man, greed, which urges him to make money or finance an end in itself. This is because man generally does not seek to have at his disposal what is necessary to lead a virtuous life, but rather to have an infinite means that satisfies the infinite insatiability of his whim; hence, he tries to accumulate artificial wealth, money, gold, with which he can capriciously acquire whatever his whim demands.

This is why man accumulates unlimited, infinite money and he seeks to increase it, not through the production of natural wealth. to, but rather by itself. Money begets more money, either by the exchange of one metal for another, or—which is much more intolerable—with the *foenus* or loan at interest, or usury. "And so," says Aristotle, "there is a kind of generation when money increases from money."[a] It is as if

a Meinvielle does not give a precise citation in Aristotle; however, the text that appears above is actually found in Aquinas' commentary: Thomas Aquinas, *Commentary on Aristotle's Politics,* trans. Richard J. Regan (Indianapolis: Hackett Publishing, 2007), 60.

money had a baby. I have $100, and at the end of the year, automatically, without the intervention of my work, by virtue of the innate fertility of money, I have 105 in my hands. You personally don't have to work to be rich. The others will work, it is true, but for my benefit, so that my money will have offspring.

LOAN AT INTEREST

Before offering an exposition of the understanding that capitalism has forged of money, and the resources that it has used to infallibly ensure its productivity, let us see why both the Mosaic law and Christian legislation have prohibited usury or interest that is charged for money borrowed.

Here, I am not talking about exaggerated interest, for example, 30 percent which is called usury today, and which would be an abuse of usury, but rather of any interest, even if it is only 1/2 percent, and which is what was always known as usury.

The Church always condemned usury as unjust and nefarious. Let us cite just a few documents.

In 1139, the First Lateran Council, in canon 13, says: "*We condemn that practice accounted despicable and blameworthy by divine and human laws, denounced by Scripture in the Old and New Testaments, namely, the ferocious greed of usurers.*"[7,b]

Clement V (in the 14th century), in the Constitution *Ex gravi ad nos* teaches: "*If indeed someone has fallen into the error of presuming to affirm pertinaciously that the practice of usury is not sinful, we decree that he is to be punished as a heretic.*"[c] However, the greatest document in this matter is the encyclical *Vix pervenit*, by Benedict XIV, precisely in 1745, when capitalism

7 See note 3 at the end of this book.

b First Lateran Council, *Canons*.

c Council of Vienne, "Ex Gravi Ad Nos" (Decree), 29.

was quickly taking off; this encyclical was directed against the errors of the Calvinists, who authorized usury.

The Holy Father declared:

> The nature of the sin called usury has its proper place and origin in a loan contract. This financial contract between consenting parties demands, by its very nature, that one return to another only as much as he has received. The sin rests on the fact that sometimes the creditor desires more than he has given. Therefore he contends some gain is owed him beyond that which he loaned, but any gain which exceeds the amount he gave is illicit and usurious.
>
> One cannot condone the sin of usury by arguing that the gain is not great or excessive, but rather moderate or small; neither can it be condoned by arguing that the borrower is rich; nor even by arguing that the money borrowed is not left idle, but is spent usefully, either to increase one's fortune, to purchase new estates, or to engage in business transactions. The law governing loans consists necessarily in the equality of what is given and returned; once the equality has been established, whoever demands more than that violates the terms of the loan. Therefore if one receives interest, he must make restitution according to the commutative bond of justice; its function in human contracts is to assure equality for each one. This law is to be observed in a holy manner. If not observed exactly, reparation must be made.
>
> By these remarks, however, We do not deny that at times together with the loan contract certain

other titles-which are not at all intrinsic to the contract-may run parallel with it. From these other titles, entirely just and legitimate reasons arise to demand something over and above the amount due on the contract. Nor is it denied that it is very often possible for someone, by means of contracts differing entirely from loans, to spend and invest money legitimately either to provide oneself with an annual income or to engage in legitimate trade and business. From these types of contracts honest gain may be made.

There are many different contracts of this kind. In these contracts, if equality is not maintained, whatever is received over and above what is fair is a real injustice. Even though it may not fall under the precise rubric of usury (since all reciprocity, both open and hidden, is absent), restitution is obligated. Thus if everything is done correctly and weighed in the scales of justice, these same legitimate contracts suffice to provide a standard and a principle for engaging in commerce and fruitful business for the common good. Christian minds should not think that gainful commerce can flourish by usuries or other similar injustices. On the contrary We learn from divine Revelation that justice raises up nations; sin, however, makes nations miserable.

But you must diligently consider this, that some will falsely and rashly persuade themselves-and such people can be found anywhere-that together with loan contracts there are other legitimate titles or, excepting loan contracts, they might convince themselves that other just contracts exist, for which it is permissible to receive a

> moderate amount of interest. Should any one think like this, he will oppose not only the judgment of the Catholic Church on usury, but also common human sense and natural reason.[d]

Thus far the encyclical of Benedict XIV.

This document clearly expresses the doctrine of the Church at that exact moment when it will cease to influence men's economic relations.

The modern economic system, inspired by the anti-Catholic spirit of the Protestant Reformation, especially that of Calvin and that of the Puritans, not only authorizes but also glorifies usury by making lending at interest the circulatory system of economic life.

Capitalism arises, great and glorious. The most formidable industrial progress on the face of the earth is made as the effect of interest-bearing loans that have become a permanent institution. In this economy, money is fertile, productive, with offspring.

Faced with this new reality that the facts present, the Church maintains (and does not reject) her sempiternal doctrine and allows her children (Canon 1543 of Canon Law[e]) to receive the legal interest on the loans of money or fungible things. This is not because she has forgotten or changed her doctrine, but rather, in response to new realities that she

---

d Benedict XIV, "Vix Pervenit" (Encyclical, Rome, November 1, 1745).

e The 1917 Code of Canon Law. The text reads: "If a fungible thing is given to another so that it becomes his, and later it must be restored in the same sort, no profit can by made by reason of the contract; but in the loan of a fungible thing, it is not by itself illicit to reap a legal profit, unless it can be shown to be immoderate of itself, and even greater profit [can be made] if there is a just and proportionate title so supporting." Eng. trans. from Edward N. Peter, *The 1917 Pio-Benedictine Code of Canon Law in English* (San Francisco: Ignatius Press, 2001), 516.

cannot change at the moment, the Church allows her children to take advantage of the universal productivity of money.[8]

In raising this question, here the legality in conscience for those who currently live in the modern economic regime is dispensed with, and the question arises:

Is a system of economy, based on lending at interest, in itself fair and beneficial?

Wouldn't such a system, even if it undergoes some grandiose development, turn out to be disastrous, since it cannot serve the human well-being of the community? Will not the grandeur of such a system necessarily benefit some at the expense of the social body?

ILLICITNESS OF A LOAN AT INTEREST

Why did Mosaic law and Christian legislation always severely forbid usury? Saint Thomas replies: *Usury is not a sin because it is prohibited, but it is prohibited because it is a sin: "To take usury for money lent is unjust in itself, because this is to sell what does not exist, and this evidently leads to inequality which is contrary to justice."*[9] It is as if I, without selling anything, were to charge $5. I give $0 and receive $5. This would obviously be unfair. Indeed, this is precisely what happens with usury, that is, the rent or the interest received for the loan of money or of something consumable.

Saint Thomas continues:

> In order to make this evident, we must observe that there are certain things, the use of which consists in their consumption: thus we consume wine when we use it for drink and we consume wheat when we use it for food. Wherefore in such

8 See Appendix I at the end on "Lending at Interest and the Conduct of the Church."

9 Cf. ST II-II, q. 78, a. 1, and *De Malo*, q. 13, 4. The citation here and the one that follows is from the *Summa* text.

> like things the use of the thing must not be reckoned apart from the thing itself, and whoever is granted the use of the thing, is granted the thing itself and for this reason, to lend things of this kin is to transfer the ownership. Accordingly if a man wanted to sell wine separately from the use of the wine, he would be selling the same thing twice, or he would be selling what does not exist, wherefore he would evidently commit a sin of injustice. On like manner he commits an injustice who lends wine or wheat, and asks for double payment, viz. one, the return of the thing in equal measure, the other, the price of the use, which is called usury.
>
> On the other hand, there are things the use of which does not consist in their consumption: thus to use a house is to dwell in it, not to destroy it. Wherefore in such things both may be granted: for instance, one man may hand over to another the ownership of his house while reserving to himself the use of it for a time, or vice versa, he may grant the use of the house, while retaining the ownership. For this reason a man may lawfully make a charge for the use of his house, and, besides this, revendicate the house from the person to whom he has granted its use, as happens in renting and letting a house.

It is clear that this charge could never be considered as the rent or lease of the modern contract based on location because in this, the rent that is charges implies usuary within it, that is, interest on the capital invested. The modern concept of "rent" is a capitalist notion and hence one of usuary; let the same be said of the letting of fields.

Saint Thomas continues:

> Now money, according to the Philosopher (*Ethic.* v, 5; *Polit.* i, 3) was invented chiefly for the purpose of exchange: and consequently the proper and principal use of money is its consumption or alienation, whereby it is sunk in exchange. Hence it is by its very nature unlawful to take payment for the use of money lent, which payment is known as usury.

According to this doctrine, it should be said that money in itself, that is, by its very nature, is sterile, infertile. Hence, it is unjust to charge for a loan as if it were fertile, as if it produced, as if it had offspring.

For this reason, in the Mosaic law the Lord ordered the Jews: "You shall not demand interest from your kindred on a loan of money or of food or of anything else which is loaned. From a foreigner you may demand interest, but you may not demand interest from your kindred, so that the LORD, your God, may bless you in all your undertakings on the land you are to enter and possess."[10]

Of course, someone will say that if the Jews were permitted to loan at interest to foreigners, then it is not something evil in itself. The Angelic Doctor replies:

> The Jews were forbidden to take usury from their brethren, i.e. from other Jews. By this we are given to understand that to take usury from any man is evil simply, because we ought to treat every man as our neighbor and brother, especially in the state of the Gospel, whereto all are called. . . . They were permitted, however, to take usury from foreigners, not as though it were lawful, but in order to avoid a greater evil, lest, to wit, through

10 Dt 23:20-21 (Meinvielle cites 23:19)

> avarice to which they were prone according to Isaiah 56:11, they should take usury from the Jews who were worshippers of God.[11]

Hence the Church always prohibited usury or lending at interest. She only authorized it in exceptional cases, and not because of the fertility that was attributed to money itself, but because of certain causes extrinsic to money itself, such as the damages that in certain and determined cases loaning money might entail. Legalized usury was officially introduced with the Reformation, and above all with Calvinism. As the Catholic understanding or influence diminishes, usury grows. But let's not get ahead of ourselves.

Summarizing the above, it turns out that the doctrines of Aristotle and Saint Thomas, the eminently Catholic doctrine regarding finance, can be summarized in the following points:

1. Only the products of the land and industry are true wealth.
2. Money is an instrument of exchange, whose value is based on natural wealth that can be purchased with it.
3. By its very nature, money is absolutely infertile; it has no right to offspring.
4. Therefore, usury or interest, whatever it may be, received on a loan is unjust.

MONEY IN CAPITALISM

Capitalism will invert the whole of this very clear doctrine, since it will make money into a commodity; indeed, it will make money the only commodity or wealth, riches that mathematically proliferate as time passes.

For this, capitalism's commitment—unconscious but real and deep—will be reduced to providing a monetary instrument that allows it to be as detached as possible from

11 ST II-II, q. 78, a. 1, ad 2.

natural wealth and to produce money with money, proliferate money: this instrument will be gold with its innumerable substitutes.

As money, gold will not have value insofar as it is representative of all the natural wealth of a nation, but rather an intrinsic value, the only one that is desirable. Hence, gold will become the only desirable wealth, because all other riches will be sought only insofar as they can be reduced to gold.

In other words, money will not be sought as a means that provides us with natural riches, but rather natural riches will be exploited as means that supply us with gold. Gold will be not a simple commodity, but rather the great commodity, *the immutable pole in the race of phenomena, the absolute measure of values.*[12]

Thus, gold is money with characteristics that are completely opposed to those that currency should have according to the wisdom of the ancients. The ancients tolerated currency as a commodity, provided that this commodity had a real value that fully coincided with its value of representation or equivalence. They assumed in this case that this currency was a circulating commodity, invariable in itself, whose variability could only originate from the variability of natural products. In other words, if products were scarce, they should go up in price; if they were abundant, they should go down in price.

However, capitalism, which makes gold the only good, begins by withdrawing it from circulation and burying it in the basements of the big banks.

Nevertheless, gold will also be the most variable of all things.[13]

12 It is the absolute measurement of values, not because it does not permit variability but because it is what is ultimately desired. Ferdinand Fried, *La Fin du Capitalisme*, 48.

13 Irving Fisher, *L'illusion de la monnaie stable.*

Variable gold tends to be pushed out of circulation; it will be replaced by other means of payment that will maintain a relationship of equivalence with gold: either paper money or checks.[14] Paper money and checks that ensure a greater circulation of the means of payment do not have a value of representation with respect to natural wealth but rather a value of representation with respect to gold. This representation value will vary according to variations in its volume.

In this way, the prices of all things are a function of three variables: gold, paper money (and checks), and natural wealth itself. Likewise, gold is also a function of three variables.[15]

MONEY TRADING

The money trade, so strongly disapproved of by the wisdom of the ancients, will be the preferred occupation of financiers who have found an easy means of enriching themselves by speculating on this infinite variability of gold, of the paper that replaces gold, and of all the other riches that will be represented on paper.

People have become so accustomed to this commercialization of money and all other economic values that it seems logical and inoffensive. However, it is not so, since all this commercialization presupposes the formation of fantastic fortunes, which are created artificially, without the real production of wealth, therefore at the expense of real production. In addition, this creates an extremely great instability for the productive forces, which must redound to the detriment of consumers and producers to benefit, instead, the speculations of the financiers.

14 See note 4 at the end of the book.

15 See note 5 at the end of this book.

MULTIPLYING MONEY

However, this is not the worst. What is serious, what is very serious about capitalist finance, is that in it money, gold, and all other values, as reducible to currency, must necessarily be fruitful. All wealth must bear interest. It is impossible to think of unproductive wealth. The money has the right to interest, to offspring. At the end of the year, one hundred pesos must necessarily become one hundred and five, for instance.

I am referring, therefore, to interest, to usury (the usury-system, legalized, at 5 percent, or 1 or 1/2 percent if you like), which in reality forms the most essential core of capitalism, because it is the concrete expression of greed.

Let us begin by noting that the notion of a loan at interest, or sale at interest, on credit, is at the root of everything; the notion of owed interest invades everything, from our mother's house, to this money, this garden, this stationary machine, everything that has a value, everything that could produce money again and does not produce it, everything is capital that can and must produce, it must have offspring. It must do so constantly and, as time passes, it increases by 4, 5, 6, 7, 8 percent, depending on the legal rate.[16]

This is actually the capitalist understanding of capital, of money. For the capitalist, there is no dead wealth: any money, thing, or good, must proliferate to the benefit of its owner, whether or not the owner has in fact produced that wealth, whether or not the work of its owner has been involved in its production.

The capitalist has one hundred dollars, but at the end of the year he is absolutely certain that it is 105, for example. There has been a foolproof, mathematical increase, an offspring of 5 dollars. An agricultural industrialist has had a splendid year and has reaped a profit of $100,000. He can now rest for life, because this year's harvest—without being

16 Malcor, "L'économie contemporaine : le crédit ou l''usure'."

consumed—with only its annual offspring, that is, with its interest, will sustain him for the rest of his life.

MONEY AND CAPITAL

Before showing the perversity of this understanding of money (as well as other wealth that is translatable into money), I will maintain that it is necessary to distinguish between money and capital.

Money is an instrument of exchange; it is made in order to be used in order to secure exchanges. It is not wealth, but rather a nominal value of wealth.

Capital, on the other hand, is a means of producing new wealth. As was explained in the previous chapter, capital is the investment of wealth in a business so that, associated to work as an instrument of production, it participates in the risks and benefits of the business. The owner of this capital, who risks this wealth in the production of new wealth, is entitled to the benefits of it. For this reason, the ancients and Saint Thomas expressly affirm that:

> He who lends money transfers the ownership of the money to the borrower. Hence the borrower holds the money at his own risk and is bound to pay it all back: wherefore the lender must not exact more. On the other hand he that entrusts his money to a merchant or craftsman so as to form a kind of society, does not transfer the ownership of his money to them, for it remains his, so that at his risk the merchant speculates with it, or the craftsman uses it for his craft, and consequently he may lawfully demand as something belonging to him, part of the profits derived from his money.[17]

17 ST II-II, q. 78, a. 2, ad 5.

Clearly, this authentic understanding of capital, accepted at all times by the Church, does not correspond with the understanding of capital in capitalism, since capitalism injects the notion of capital with interest as well. This is so true that in industrial businesses the interest on capital is not taken out of the net profit of the company, but is considered a general expense that must be deducted from the gross profit. That interest, its offspring, is something inseparable from capital. If, once the amortization of capital and its interest has been assured, there is still liquid benefit, welcome! Capital will benefit from it in the form of a dividend.

This understanding of capital is clearly unfair and usurious, as I will now demonstrate. Let us remember for now the Catholic understanding of capital, of genuine capital, as I explained in the third chapter. It is the investment of unconsumed wealth in a company, so that, associated with work as an instrument of production, it participates in the risks and benefits of the company.

Hence, we can say: 1) Capital is only an instrumental cause in production; 2) The only one who is entitled to the benefit of capital is the one associated with work; 3) The right to benefit is secondary, as it comes after work, just as its influence on production is secondary and after work; 4) Just as it is associated with work in the participation of profit, so it is also associated with risks and losses.

Hence, the principal is not entitled to any interest; nor does it have the right to deduct the amortization of capital from the gross profit, as a general expense. Capital is only entitled to the dividend in case there are liquid profits. The liquid benefit must be computed after fully satisfying the labor rights of the executor and the worker.

Only in this way will there be a true association of capital in the company, as food for work, according to the principles of Saint Thomas, as explained in the third chapter.

Now, in the event that the capital is not associated but is

rather lent, then it is only entitled to claim the full return of the capital, no matter the fate of the company, just as if you do not share in the risk of the business, you cannot claim any share in the profits.

Capitalist *capital* implies the following injustices: 1) It is considered as borrowed, and for this reason it demands its amortization, with industrial income; 2) It considers itself as associated, and claims participation in the liquid benefit; 3) It is considered as superior to work, and claims its amortization, benefit, and dividend, before the rights of work.

For this reason, it is necessary to choose either associated capital or borrowed money. It is either one or the other: choosing both, as it happens in the current type of capitalist company, it is unfair. Indeed, it is theft.

LENDING AT INTEREST IN CAPITALISM

Now, if the money is *loaned*, the interest that the capital claims as due is in fact theft. By virtue of what, if 100 dollars were given, can 105 dollars be claimed at the end of the year? Those five dollars, which are demanded by the one loaning, by virtue of what are they demanded? Because of the past year? However, is there a right to trade over time, over the year, and to charge five dollars simply because a year has passed?

Some will argue: But, the other person benefited from the money I lent him! The money was lent; hence, the money was given precisely so that it might be used. The money was given as was its use, since the two remain inseparably together. Now then, when the borrower returns the borrowed money, he also returns its use, that is, he returns everything that was given to him. The one who loans is not entitled to any benefit as he does not have to answer for any losses since, by lending the money, he let go of it. If he had not loaned the money, but rather had associated it in a business with someone else's work, the one loaning the money could justly claim a share in the profits, just as the one loaning was exposed to risks.

However, in this case it would not be borrowed money but associated: even then, the one loaning would not have any right to an *infallible amortization.*

This is a very clear and clean doctrine, which is difficult for us to understand because we have the capitalist mentality regarding money and capital.

The interest charged by the lender is wealth that has been appropriated without work. But, since it is wealth, it is the product of work, but of the work of the producer, not of the one loaning it, who produces for himself and for the one loaning. The loaner robs the producer of a part of his work. This, which clearly appears in industrial income and in modern farm income (I say *modern* because today the rental of houses and fields implies the understanding that money and capital have the right to generated income), appears more evident in the loans of the state, because the state that obtains a loan generally does not invest that money in productive works but rather in consumable or better destructible works. Hence there is a need to repay principal and interest.

The money is lent by the person who has it, that is, the financier, who is then enriched with the interest from the borrowed money. Since the state does not produce, then it is necessary to take from the producer a part of what he produces in order to pass it on and deliver it to the financier. In this way, the one who in fact makes the loan is the producer or worker, of the intellect or of the hands, but a worker nonetheless. The one who benefits—infallibly—is the non-worker, the idler, the financier.

With state loans, the state is officially in charge of passing the wealth from the hands of the producer to the hands of the non-producer.

With the loans contracted abroad, wealth is passed from the hands of the country's producers into the hands of non-producers, from abroad.

LOANS AT INTEREST DIVIDE HUMANITY INTO THE OLIGARCHY AND THE MISERABLE MULTITUDE

Lending at interest is disastrous because it divides humanity into two classes: a billionaire oligarchy that does not produce and a miserable multitude that produces.

Everything that has been said so far about finances, currency, the injustice and inconvenience of usury, must seem disjointed on the one hand, and extremely ineffective on the other. This is because, even assuming that usury had its drawbacks, is it not true that these would be more than compensated by the magnificent development achieved by industry and commerce, a development that almost entirely has to be attributed to the powerful lever of finance? and credit? Well then: I will demonstrate—reproducing the demonstration of La Tour de Pin,[18] made 40 years ago—that credit and usury are essentially nefarious, and that they have placed the modern economy in the abyss of its final grave.

Indeed: even if it is 1/2 percent, usury is a disastrous injustice, because it alone, regardless of any other cause, automatically tends to divide humanity in two large and distinct classes: one, the hoarders of money, who each day increase their money without working; the other group, those without money, who work harder every day to enrich the financial class.

The reason for this is that the interest received from the borrowed money, whether from industrial income, land rent, state loans, or simple bank loans, is taken from the hands of the producer and placed in the hands of the non-producer. In this way, each day the capital of the financier increases, and above all that of the primary financier, which is usually the world financier.

As capital increases, interest on it increases; thus, each day the part that the producer must surrender to the financier is

18 La Tour du Pin, *Vers un ordre social Chretien.*

greater.

The producer must necessarily become poorer, until a time comes when what he produces daily is not even enough to satisfy the part he owes to the interests of the financier. He goes, then, into debt and will be financially under the clutches of the financier.

Now, this is not fantasy: it is the current economic reality of the world. On the one hand we see a small number of financiers who have a huge mountain of money concentrated in their hands. On the other hand, one sees nations, industries, businesses, individuals, laden with debt, working (or attempting to work) to fulfill the enormous commitments made. For whom do you work?

For the benefit of the financier, who must suck up, until who knows what generation, the sweat of our work. The one who does not work, does not produce; all his work is artificial, financial, speculative.

IT IS NEFARIOUS BECAUSE IT GENERATES A NEFARIOUS MOUNTAIN OF MONEY

Indeed, will that mountain of money held by global financiers be left idle? Impossible, because if it is not set into action, it will not increase with interest.

But where can it be set into action, if the current producers do not offer sufficient guarantees to meet the debts contracted, and furthermore, if their manufactured products do not find markets where they can be sold?

If credit is not requested, then it is offered. Money must infallibly increase. Hence we see how in 1928 and 1929 the financiers agreed to lend 8.5 billion dollars to New York brokers for their stock speculations.[19] Credits lifted all stock values. Prosperity returned.

19 Emile Mireaux, *Les Miracles du Crédit*; Lucius, *Faillite du capitalisme?*; Fried, *La Fin du Capitalisme*.

However, this was a speculative rise. The increase was not based on a higher yield of production but rather on false speculation, which raised the values because it had money to speculate. When reality set in, it was a brutal bankruptcy.

Pierre Lucius[20] shows in statistics the course of quotations from 1923 to 1931:

Index of variable interest securities
Index of the General Statistics of France (base 1913:100)

1st Period of Increase

	Paris	New York
Minimum 1923	173	119
Maximum 1929	507	403
Increase calculated in %	195	239

2nd Period of Decrease

	Paris	New York
Minimum 1929	507	403
Maximum 1931	249	154
Decrease calculated in %	150	209

This artificially provoked boom brought about the bankruptcy of large speculators and caused the loss of the public's small savings. As a result, Hatry and Horn went bankrupt in London; Oustric, Devilder, Homberg, Bauer Marchal, and Aero-Postal in Paris; Gualino, Pánzarasa, and Brudarelli in Turin and Milan.

Why was this enormous amount of money thrown into the world's main stock exchanges, if not to make it prolific, since it is inconceivable that it remain idle without increasing?

The same can be said of the overproduction of raw materials in all the overseas countries and of industrial overproduction in the industrial countries. With its mad desire to increase, money has streamlined the United States,

20 Lucius, *Faillite du capitalisme?*, 8.

Germany, and Russia; it has brought about extraordinary progress in industry in all countries and even in previously exclusively consumer countries such as India, the Balkans, China, and the like.

Calculate the disastrous disruption of this unbridled overproduction by taking into account that each of these countries can virtually supply world consumption.

What has been the subsequent result of the agricultural-industrial expansion caused by the enormous mountain of money that rushed over the world in the mad desire to increase wealth?

Very simple: The overproduced raw materials must be stored; they are devaluated below their cost price, and in this way the peasant population ended up being submerged in misery and bankruptcy.

The industrial overproduction produced the stopping of the plants with the unemployment of the workers and the industrial bankruptcy.

"Thus in the world economy we see, on the one hand, the countrymen impoverished, unable to buy manufactured goods, machines, and tools; and on the other, the impoverished working masses who cannot satisfy their needs for raw materials."[21]

A TYPICAL CASE AMONG US

In order to appreciate the disastrous upheavals that an enormous mass of money must necessarily produce in a saturated market (that is, in a market that does not allow production yields to increase), which cannot remain idle in the hands of financiers, let us suppose that there is a financial consortium with 1,000,000,000 dollars. Financial business X has 1,000,000,000 dollars, and does not know which business or industry to give it to because no one requests it.

21 Fried, *La Fin du Capitalisme*, 22.

Will you keep this huge sum inert? By no means! It will cause prolific business in the short term, which will reimburse you with a prolific profit for said sum. However, since these businesses will not correspond to a real need of consumers, this profit will be made at the expense of owners and producers, who will have to succumb in the commercial fight, victims of the X financial consortium which will grow dizzyingly.

Suppose that Financial Group X sees a profitable business in the short term in the construction of skyscrapers. Then he will order the investment of money in that direction, not because in Buenos Aires there is a need for these houses, since the population has not increased enough for such a density, but because he sees, thanks to the snobbery of the people who like the latest apartment, their homes will be preferred at the expense of others who will be sacrificed.

In this way, Financial Consortium X, using its omnipotent power of its 1,000,000,000 dollars, will bankrupt the other owners and will cause a forced drop in rents.

The financial capacity of Financial Consortium X will not have been exhausted with this. Taking advantage of the dilapidated state of many warehouses, bakeries, fur shops, pharmacies, shirt shops, shops in the city, it will buy them at an insignificant price and will transform them, giving them an attractive and novel appearance. With this chain of model businesses scattered at strategic points in the city, it will do great business, while all the other merchants will go bankrupt. Hence, mathematically, Financial Consortium X will go about, getting its hands on everything in the Republic. Grains, cattle, milk, bread, medicine, ranches, large rented buildings, everything will pass to the X Financial Consortium, which will make enormous profits at the expense of the ruinous state of the producers and merchants, its debtors.

But are the profits of the Financial Consortium X fair? In no way. The members of the Consortium are people who operate honestly within the capitalist economy. They have money and they lend it. By lending it, they increase it with interest. So, with the loan at interest, they receive the fruits of the labor of all those who know no other way to enrich themselves than with the sweat of their brow. When these, for one reason or another, cannot meet the debts contracted, they see the need to make an arrangement with the X Financial Consortium, which usually opens itself very kindly to an understanding with the unfortunate debtor.

And what injustice is there in all this? Isn't this the logic of an economy founded on lending at interest?

Thus by logic, capitalism has become a total mess, and naive people wonder where is the money?

Where was it supposed to be? In the hands of its owners, the international financiers. Are they guilty then? Of course not.

Doesn't the modern world, the capitalist economic system, say that everything is progressing thanks to the wonders of credit?

How can we be surprised then at the fact that the creditors have in their hands all the money in the world? If they have collected it lawfully, it is because the producers have agreed to give it to them!

"MORE MONEY IS NEEDED"

But, if they have money, why don't they release it into circulation?

And for what end? To increase production? But the current production is already excessive. To increase consumption?

But in this case, with what guarantees would they be able to offer it to consumers, if consumers would not be able to repay it?

Who will put their money into circulation now, if there are no guarantees of productivity? Furthermore, if it were put into circulation, the phenomenon of 1929 stock market disaster would be repeated.

Besides, if the lenders put their money into circulation, they would feel a momentary, artificial relief, which would later bring about a more desperate situation. By collecting the money with its corresponding offspring, the producer would produce for the benefit of the financier; hence, the financier would be richer and the world poorer, constantly aggravating the evil.

MONEY, SIMPLY AN INSTRUMENT OF EXCHANGE

Nonetheless, it is true that money is needed, *an instrument of exchange*, a pure instrument of exchange that puts goods and merchandise into circulation. However, it is not necessary (indeed, it would be very harmful) that money or capital has the right to offspring, to usury.

Hence, the money that is needed is money that does not produce offspring, money that has been exorcised from usury, even from legal percentage usury. What is needed is money as Aristotle and Saint Thomas wanted it.

This is the only solution to the world's economic problem; the demonstration formulated is of a fatal mathematical rigor. It is a solution that is not wanted and that has not even been glimpsed; it is a solution that, even if it were to be glimpsed, would not be applied because, as the world is ruled by global financiers, they would never allow a solution that destroys their exclusive interests.

Traditional philosophy provides the only possible solution to the world's economic crisis. Meanwhile, the celebrities of economics and politics get worked up, determined to cure the comatose state of the economic organism with the very treatments that have brought it to that state.

USURY AS VICE, USURY AS SYSTEM

Usury is therefore unfair and harmful. The current crisis, the definitive one for capitalism, is the first effect of usury.

Some will claim that vicious usury is only that of an exaggerated interest, but not of legal usury, that is, of the modest usury that honest banks receive.

However, I ask: once usury is justified and legalized, who will keep it on fair terms, if by its nature it keeps increasing? Furthermore, where does legal usury end and vicious usury begin? Don't the financiers impose the rate of their loans and the state legalizes it with its acceptance?

However, setting aside all this, even if it were true that the current economic paralysis was not due simply to credit but to the abuse of credit, is it not in any case true that credit will only have hastened, accelerated the disastrous effects of usury, and that even without this abuse, albeit more slowly but with the same mathematical infallibility, this disastrous state would have been reached?

Our proof cannot be avoided. It is of a fatal mathematical rigor, I repeat. Mathematical rigor that still explains the apparent orderly use of credit in the growth of capitalism and the disorderly use in these last years of its heyday. It is like a moving body that, as it approaches its center of gravity, increases its speed; usury and its deadly effects were to increase as capitalism reached its apogee. Usury, then, has destroyed capitalism.

There is yet another objection. If usury has always been practiced, why is it now so deadly? Isn't this just a simplistic solution to the economic crisis?

Never before has usury been practiced as a necessity of economic life. Tradition, both Judeo-Christian and Greco-Roman philosophy as well as all traditional civilizations, has always condemned usury.

It was practiced, it is true, hidden from the sight of the law, but it was this usury that brought Rome to destruction.

Therefore, now that usury has become a necessity such as previous centuries have never seen, we will also reach a catastrophe unique in world history.

Evidently, when the industrial capacity of the world had not managed to balance the real capacity of consumption, the disastrous effects of usury were not visible. Since then the production was then of positive yield, it was possible that it enriched the financier and the producer. However, now that capitalism has reached its apogee, now that the productive capacity already exceeds the consuming quantity, yield has become problematic—if not impossible—and usury appears in all its catastrophic perversity.

Chapter 5

Consumption

In the preceding chapter we have seen the fate of an economy devoted to money as its ultimate goal. Since money in itself can be infinite and unlimited, as Aristotle and Saint Thomas observed, it will necessarily imprint a movement of infinite acceleration to all economic life. This is in fact what happened. The insatiable desire for profit, a desire not only unleashed but also glorified in the modern economic regime, stimulated the trading of money with money to produce more money. Finance, with its motor of the loan at interest, crowned all economic life.

In an economy placed under the power of profit, the commerce of merchandise had to follow after finances, running dizzyingly, because in it, without a directly productive activity, money increases rapidly. As a result, commercial and mercantile life, with the unbridled fury of maritime, river, and road transport, stirs up the whole of humanity which that had been relatively peaceful until then, turning it into an immense market.

Then comes production, also in a dizzying race following after commerce in order to respond to the incessant demand of the market. First comes industrial production, because it is exercised in the domain of what is artificial and therefore of what is unlimited; secondly comes natural production since, for the same reasons, it is tied to the limited demands of natural forces.

Finally, if it is necessary to produce in order to trade and to trade in order to profit, it is also necessary to consume, because if there is no consumption, then production is not possible. However, consumption is always necessarily limited, even if it is perverted on purpose. It is also more limited than the production of the land. Hence, it must come after it.

Hence, in the lucrative economy of the modern world, consumption comes at the tail end of every economic process, dragged by production, just as production is dragged by commerce, and the latter, in turn, by banking.

It would be wrong to draw from this the consequence that in the modern world no one seeks to eat. On the contrary, what is sought is that people eat and consume in an infinite, unlimited, accelerated way, in order to be able to infinitely produce, infinitely trade, and infinitely profit. In this world without God, the infinity of matter filters through all domains of activity.

Hence, the error of the modern economy is not in suppressing consumption. On the contrary, it is in raising it to infinity to push the other economic processes to infinity as well.

In other words: the modern economy is an "inverted" economy, as I explained in the first chapter. An infinite economy together with finite man. A purely dynamic economy next to the primordially static man. A profit economy together with man who is a consumer being. This economy would suppress consumption if it was convenient for profit; the same economy would increase it to infinity if profit demanded it.

This, which may seem like a literary paradox, is history, as Marcel Malcor has shown in his wonderful studies on the contemporary economy.[1]

Indeed, when England, in the century and a half of its economic imperialism, had a million and a half clients in front of its powerful industry, of consumers scattered all over the world, it is careful not to preach theories about increases in wages and consumption, popularized today by American theory. What need can there be to increase the consumption capacity in its 20, 30 or 40 million sober Englishmen like Puritans, if it cannot supply its enormous worldwide clientele?

However, today, when the instruments of production can supply the world several times over, it is necessary to preach the need for infinite consumption. (I say: it can supply. If in fact it does not supply, it is for other reasons). From here arises Henry Ford's theory, when he teaches that "the machine lives on quantity, and since quantity is the worker himself, he is the most interesting consumer, the only interesting one. It is necessary, therefore, that his salary allow him to buy what he produces."[a]

"Industry cannot be said to be solidly established," he adds, "except when the great mass of consumers coincides with the great mass of its workers."

Since today the instruments of production are more powerful than the world's capacity for consumption, all the effort of the economy is concentrated on deifying consumption. This explains all of the words praising the increase in consumption, advertising that provokes consumption, the very fast fashion that rushes consumption, and consumer credit, which accelerates it.

1 Malcor, "L'économie contemporaine," Malcor, "L'économie contemporaine : travail, assurances, capitalisme," Malcor, "L'économie contemporaine : le crédit ou l''usure'."

a No citation is given by Meinvielle.

ADVERTISING, FASHION, AND CONSUMER CREDIT

Let us briefly examine these four chapters of the contemporary economy, now bent on glorifying consumption, since only in this way will we be able to explain one of the most interesting aspects of this inverted economy, which is that, after having produced *ad nauseam*, it rushes to destroy what has been produced, because it foretells the stagnation that brings about death.

Contemporary economics formulates lengthy praises of consumption. We have already quoted Henry Ford. On the same token, it is impossible to forget the other great type of American who is ex-president Hoover: "The man who has a standard automobile, a standard radio, and an hour and a half less daily work, has a fuller life and more personality than he had before."[b]

Mr. Mellon, former US secretary of the economy, is proud of his country's capacity for consumption: "Although our population," he says, "represents less than 7 percent of the total land area, last year we consumed 48 percent of the world's coffee production, 53 percent of tin production; 65 percent of the rubber; 21 percent of the sugar; 72 percent of the silk; 36 percent of the coal; 41 percent of the iron; 47 percent of the copper; 69 percent of oil. From now on, we can expect a natural and inevitable growth of both population and natural wealth."[2]

---

2 Interview with Andrew W. Mellon, "Interview," *Evening Standard* (London), November 27, 1928. Cited in Malcor, "L'économie contemporaine : travail, assurances, capitalisme."

---

b Meinvielle gives no citation for this text. Other sources cite the text as: "The man who has a standard automobile, a standard telephone, a standard bathtub, a standard electric light, a standard radio, and one and one-half hours less average daily labor is more of a man and has a fuller life and more individuality than he has without them." Cited in Vinsel, *Moving Violations: Automobiles, Experts, and Regulations in the United States*, 58.

The satisfaction of these civilized barbarians, who imagine that the increase of the population and of the natural wealth depends on gluttony, makes us laugh. For them consumption is the measure of civilization. For this reason, the United States, which drinks half of the coffee produced in the world, is more civilized than Europe, just as Europe is much more civilized than the East.

If man is an eminently consuming animal, it is necessary to encourage him to consume products whose consumption dignifies him so much. However, first man must understand the convenience of adapting himself to this permanent incitement, of being interested by advertising. For this reason, the many advertising companies educate modern man by urgently showing him the serious interest that reading advertisements implies. "Read this." "Get used to reading these notices," they tell you. The recommendation is, on the other hand, utterly useless, because the assault of American advertising, with a thousand unimaginable resources, attacks all the senses, makes use of all the senses, reaches into the heart, and finally numbs the spirit.

Advertising is always in direct proportion to the uselessness of the item. Thus, the Wrigley company spends 4,000,000 dollars of the 16,000,000 that it sells in chewing gum for advertising. It is easy to verify that the more artificial a product is, the more it is advertised, the more effective for others: "because in modern man, desire is subject to the laws of mechanics; repetition, a certain intensity, automatically loosens his rope at the price of an easily calculable expense and that can comfortably figure, in advance, in the calculation of the price."[3] This is why it is easy to discover the philosophical meaning of the enormous warning waste: in the current understanding of life, man is a consuming animal lost

3 See Malcor, "L'économie contemporaine."

in an impersonal mass; it is necessary, therefore, to act on his five senses in order to encourage him to consume.

If man is a consuming animal, because, in the modern understanding, he is a concrete being of pure matter subject to the laws of mechanics, then he must be endowed, like matter, with continuous mobility; this is because the local, transient movement that the scholastics claim is opposed to the immanent, and that modern man calls activity, energy, dynamism, is an inevitable consequence of matter. For this, it is necessary to progress, to have a makeover, to quickly renew consumption, and to deify fashion. It is necessary to eat, drink, dress, play, live, and behave in accord with fashion.

Fashion, which was previously reserved for the aristocracy as an expression of beauty, has today invaded all domains and all social classes. It is an effective conquest of democracy.

"It is remarkable," says Marcel Malcor, "that the concern of fashion (which once did not go beyond a very restricted medium) is today totally generalized and popularized. All efforts of advertising, which here is king above all, are directed towards the masses. Two things are important to it: that the change be frequent enough, as frequent as possible, and that it can be adopted uniformly, almost instantaneously, from top to bottom, in the scale of fortunes... under the original form or that of a substitute."[4]

However, the considerations regarding consumption and its permanent incitement would be of no use if the possibility of consuming was not facilitated for man. For this, consumer credit has been organized as the most natural thing in the world. "The normal mode of sale—especially in the United States—of a car, a phonograph, a chair, a spoon, is by monthly payments. All active sectors of the economy have organized sales on credit chronically, regularly and in view of a rapid progression. According to a sympathetic observer from the

4 Malcor, "L'économie contemporaine."

United States, the floating credit of trade on retail customers is 7 billion of dollars (1926); the public is always a year behind with respect to their income."[5]

INVERTED CONSUMPTION

It is impossible to make it any clearer that economic concern is now focused on the acceleration of consumption.

It is a pernicious acceleration: because with it what is being sought is that man spend simply in order to spend. Indeed, the goal is that man spend above all on what is useless, on entertainment, whims, on luxuries that do not match his social condition. Recall, for instance, the popularization of silk stockings and makeup among women, and the like.

In reality, the consumption of the contemporary economy is quite the opposite of the consumption of an economy ordered according to natural requirements. In this natural economy, consumption is the purpose of economic life. What is produced is to provide man with what he needs for a human life, within his condition, as Saint Thomas said.[6] Consumption is ordered according to the human requirements of each person's life. There is a deep sense of hierarchy. In turn, consumption regulates trade, currency, and production as an end. The economy is placed under the mark of what is human; the economy serves man just as man, on his part, serves God.

However, someone will object: does bringing this up not imply an obvious setback in the unbending march of humanity that runs towards progress? Humanity runs so hard that it's about to crash.

As there is an inversion, as we said, in the economic process, consumption is itself perverted. What is consumed is consumed badly, and it is consumed badly so that the merchant can liquidate his stocks with profits, the producers

5 Malcor, "L'économie contemporaine : le crédit ou l'‘usure’."

6 ST II-II, q. 118, a. 1.

can speed up their machines, and the bankers can multiply their productive credits.

It is so true that consumption drags down the entire economic process, that it is preferable to destroy enormous amounts of coffee, corn, wheat, and such, in order to ensure profit, rather than feed the millions of starving people.

Again, this is the logic of an economy that has forgotten the elementary law of economic life as laid about by Saint Thomas: "In all things that are for an end, the good consists in a certain measure: since whatever is directed to an end must needs be commensurate with the end .... External goods come under the head of things useful for an end. Hence it must needs be that man's good in their respect consists in a certain measure, in other words, that man seeks, according to a certain measure, to have external riches, insofar as they are necessary for him to live in keeping with his condition of life."[7] Cardinal Cajetan comments: "with the word *life*, he understands not only food and drink but everything that is fitting and delightful, within what is honest."

Therefore, the proximate law of economic life must be that man's consumption should be according to his condition.

What is produced, is produced in order to be consumed... it is traded in order to be consumed... money is used as a means of circulating wealth that ensures a more abundant and varied consumption.

Profit as such (the only law of modern economics) is always severely condemned in a Christian economy. This is so true that at the time of the Fathers of the Church (1st to 7th centuries)—in order to react against the purely lucrative spirit of the pagan economy—mercantilism, where profit is preferably sought, was rejected.

In his first letter to Timothy, Saint Paul says (6:6-10):

---

7 ST II-II, q. 118, a. 1.

> Indeed, religion with contentment is a great gain. For we brought nothing into the world, just as we shall not be able to take anything out of it. If we have food and clothing, we shall be content with that. Those who want to be rich are falling into temptation and into a trap and into many foolish and harmful desires, which plunge them into ruin and destruction. For the love of money is the root of all evils, and some people in their desire for it have strayed from the faith and have pierced themselves with many pains.

To many, this text will seem of ascetic but not economic value; to them, on the contrary, it will seem destructive of the economy. However, this is not the case. It is an eminently economic text, because precisely the last verse explains to us the anti-economic character of an alleged economy regulated by greed: it separates man from faith, that is, from the Christian life, and immerses him body and soul in purely economic concerns (first error). It subjects him to many penalties, because it does not provide him with economic well-being; on the contrary, it enslaves him, as contemporary economics demonstrates (second error).

The very well-being of the economy requires, as far as possible, the expulsion of profit, and a movement that curbs all those activities that, due to their own inclination, tend to profit, such as commerce and finance.

For this reason, unlike the pagan writers who justified big business and judged small industry and small trade as unworthy of a free man, the Fathers of the Church began from Saint Paul to rehabilitate manual work.

Saint Augustine himself writes that, if spiritual work did not take him so long, he would want to imitate Saint Paul (who worked building tents), exercising "a work as innocent as it is honest, relative to everyday objects, like those that come from the hands of blacksmiths and shoemakers, or like work in the fields."[8,c]

Indeed, work, especially that which has more contact with nature and is of a more creative nature, dignifies man, while profit from mercantile activities dulls him, making it impossible for him to achieve supernatural dignity.

COMMERCE

However, it would be wrong to condemn commerce as a bad thing in itself. Saint Thomas has known how to balance the just doctrine, when he teaches:

> There is an exchange or business of money for money, or merchandise for money, not to obtain what is necessary for life but to seek profit. And this business is that of the merchants. This trade, considered in itself, is blameworthy, because it is at the service of the concupiscence of profit, which has no end but tends to infinity. And for this reason, commerce, considered in itself, has a certain perversity, insofar as it does not have an honest or necessary end of its own. However, although in its reason it has nothing honest or necessary, the profit that is sought in commerce has in itself nothing vicious or contrary to virtue; from where nothing prevents profit or gain from being ordered to an honest or necessary purpose; and thus, trade is lawful. Like, for example, when someone orders the gain moderate who seeks in commerce to sustain his house, or to help the indigent; or also, when someone dedicates

8 Alceu Amoroso Lima, *Esbozo de una Introducción a la Economía Moderna*, 168.

c Alceu Amoroso Lima wrote using the pseudonym Tristao de Athayde.

> himself to commerce to provide for public need so that what is necessary for life is not lacking in his country, and asks for profit, not as an end but as a stipend for his work.[d]

From all this doctrine it follows that, in order to justify the profit of merchants and commerce itself, it is necessary to order it to an honest and necessary end, such as consumption. Without this arrangement, commerce is bad and detrimental, as happens in capitalism.

This is why in the modern economy, which is "industrialist" (as opposed to manual), "profitable" (as opposed to consumer), "impersonal or anonymous" (as opposed to personal), "quantitative" (as opposed to qualitative), "provocative based on claims," trade is king and banking is the emperor.

The same statistic helps demonstrate the disproportionate increase in commerce with respect to the industry itself:

> So, for instance, in France the commercial professions comprised 900,000 individuals under the second empire and today 2,700,000 (1921); that is a three-fold increase. In the same time, the industrial population had not increased by more than 1.6 times. In England, there are two merchants for every farmer. In America, it is approximately one merchant for two farmers. It's a lucrative activity.

Ferdinand Fried notes how Germany's first "new rich men," the partners Otto Wolff and Ottmar Strauss from Cologne, who are at the head of the mining industry with a fortune of 50 million gold marks each, and Peevckek, whose

d Meinvielle gives no citation, although it appears to come from the commentary on Aristotle's *Politics*.

mines of lignite (brown coal) are valued at 150 million, have found the basis of their fortune in commerce, because commerce greatly favors big profits.[9]

Industry itself has made great fortunes because it is primarily commercial, mercantile, with all the quick and easy profits that it brings.

To some this race of consumption to the drag of infinite production, infinite trade, infinite finances, will seem excessive. What does it matter, someone will ask sooner or later, if it's sufficiently insured? What does it matter, above all, if never before have we had such an immense abundance? It may be, that person will say, that this implies a moral inversion, but economically it is an effort that humanity has never achieved. The modern economy is just great.

It is known that the doctrine of the Church does not admit this divorce of values. There can be no economy, a truly economic one, that violates the hierarchy of human values. It may seem great, but it is immoral; it bears a terrifying destructive force at its roots that will finish off man and it will destroy the economy itself. If it is immoral, it is uneconomic.

Now then: the current economic reality will reveal to us, in a characteristic fact, the fulfillment of this doctrine.

THE BANKRUPTCY OF A PROFIT ECONOMY

We have said before that the supreme goal of the contemporary economy is to increase man's consumption to infinity. The very life of the economy requires it. If it manages to increase consumption so that it is on a par with its productive capacity, liberal capitalism will be saved and will continue to reign in the universe. Because, what is the economic situation in the world today? There is obviously a financial super-capacity, as was demonstrated in the fourth chapter. There is plenty of money, since it is accumulated

9 Fried, *La Fin du Capitalisme*, 80.

without being able to be handed out, invested. Finances are saturated.

The financial super-capacity is responsible for a mercantile super-capacity, saturating the world markets. All countries are today more or less self-sufficient, at least for the common type of agricultural and industrial products. When liberalism was expanding, when England exported her manufactured goods in exchange for the raw materials throughout the world, it was easy to understand commercial exchange. However, today, when everyone has production machinery and, to a large extent, raw materials, saturation has almost been achieved. This explains why the world is divided into closed economic fields. Each of them is in a position to produce for the world: the United States on one side, England on the other, Germany in third place, Russia on the prowl, and Japan in the Far East. The protectionist pace of the world is a consequence of commercial saturation.

The financial and mercantile super-capacity caused the industrial and agricultural super-capacity that is spoken of in the second and third chapters.

Now then: there is saturation, stagnation in finance, market, and industry. For this to continue forward, it is necessary for consumption to work, which comes a step behind; let consumption proceed slowly, because the other path is a runaway race.

Now then, consumption cannot, not just run, but even walk. This is because, in order for consumption to walk and run, the cost of living must be cheap and people's resources abundant.

On the contrary, the cost of living must be high, and people's resources scarce. Indeed, the cost of living is very high and the resources are very scarce, because the entire economy is inverted. I hope the proof is conclusive; in this way the perennial up-to-date-ness of Thomistic thought will also be demonstrated. Only Aquinas can diagnose the world's economic malaise and accurately predict the future.

The cost of living must be very high, because between the producer and the consumer are the financier, the merchant and the state, three entities that of their own do not produce and that consume enormously. Hence, support for them must weigh heavily on the cost of life.

In addition, there is another factor that intervenes to increase the cost, and that is the excessive division of labor. Although it could be true that the division of labor, as such, reduces the cost of the product, it is worth noting that the charges corresponding to the financier and the state in each stage of the work are added in cascades, so that they multiply by two, by three, and even by more the gross cost of a somewhat complex manufacture.[10] However, let us set aside this circumstance and stick to the fact that the financier, the merchant, and the state stand between the producer and the consumer.

Now then, the rights of the financier have been increased disproportionately both by means of public loans (the debts of the world war alone weigh on the books of the world, according to the calculations of Herr Renatus, two billion gold marks) as in terms of industrial and farm income and in terms of bank loans, at the same time that the money itself has been passing from the hand of the producer to the hands of the financier.[11] This is in regards to capital, which is considered productive.

If we take into account that there is enormous capital that now, due to industrial paralysis, does not produce and that nevertheless receives its fixed income as if it produced, the proportion increases unbelievably. Following Schmalenbach, Ferdinand Fried underlines this with respect to Germany. "We work," he says, "not only to give assistance to the 4 million unemployed but also to pay interest and amortize

10 Malcor, "L'économie contemporaine : le crédit ou l''usure'."

11 Ramiro de Maeztu, *La Prensa*, October 20, 1932.

immobilized machines, that is to guarantee their income to capital."[12]

The merchant's rights (and this includes small, medium, and large businesses, and even in this last one distinctions can be made following a visible progression from the simple importer to the powerful world monopoly) have been multiplying, and it will be easy to appreciate the enormous network of intermediaries that become wealthy without producing. I say without producing, not by way of criticism, but rather to highlight the enormous burden that must weigh upon the cost of living.

This, assuming the best of cases (a purely theoretical case), that the merchants are content with making a profit; because today they steal shamelessly, perhaps not the little trader who can't, nor the middleman who is broke, but certainly the trader who is a hoarder on a global scale.

To accomplish this, they have a perfect, unbreakable organization, which they call a consortium, cartel, concern, trust, and which is nothing other than what Aristotle calls "monopoly."[13] These monopolies freely set the cheapest possible price for the producer and the most expensive for the consumer.

In addition to the financier and the merchant, there is a dangerous parasite that stands between the producer and the consumer to make life extraordinarily expensive. It is the modern bureaucratic state, which weighs as a heavy burden on the lowly municipality and on the provincial and national levels.

The modern state today is a vulgar mutual society or a placement agency. Their budgets are huge; taxes grow every day, so that they are equivalent to simple expropriation.

---

12 Fried, *La Fin du Capitalisme*, 547, 78.

13 *Politicorum*, liber 1, c. IX.

Studying the influence of this phenomenon in the current crisis, Pierre Lucius observes how in the production of certain products the fiscal charges have increased, from 1913 to 1929, by 100 percent, and reproduces the testimony of Gastón Jéze, professor at the Faculty of Law in Paris, who says: "Deficit is the rule in England, in France, in Italy, in Germany, to cite only the great States. The cause that produces it is permanent; their influence only increases. It is the demagogic spirit."[14] Between us, this cause is easy to verify.

Now, with these three agents who devour money without producing, life must be excessively expensive. "Thorald Rogers, in a study whose objective value has never been challenged, wrote in 1880, after a long enumeration of the price of food, materials, wages, and especially building wages, in 1450: 'If the reader has the patience to do the necessary calculations, he will find that, excluding rents, my multiplier of 12 (between the price of life for 1450 and the price for 1880) is quite accurate.' With regard to Merton Tower at Oxford, he says that its cost, valued in modern currency, was then £1,630. Built today, it would cost 4,000 to 5,000 pounds. He said this in 1880. Today its cost will have to be increased by 25 percent."[15,e]

Now, while life has become more expensive, the resources of individuals (especially the worker and employee) have become scarcer.

This occurs, first, because the money was taken from them with the loan at interest, as we said in the fourth chapter, and, second, due to the phenomenon of technical progress, which determines unemployment and lower wages.

14 Lucius, *Faillite du capitalisme?*

15 Marcel Malcor, in *Nova et Vetera*.

e It is not clear which work of Malcor Meinvielle is citing: Malcor, "L'économie contemporaine," Malcor, "L'économie contemporaine : travail, assurances, capitalisme," Malcor, "L'économie contemporaine : le crédit ou l''usure'."

Hence, if life is expensive and resources are scarce, consumption cannot run, or even walk.

The modern economy, which lives on movement, must come to a standstill and die: the logical result of an "inverted" economy.

Why? This comes about because by boosting finances, money was passing from the hands of the poor to the hands of the rentier; from the hands of the producer to those of the international financier. A huge but deadly capital was created. By promoting trade and industry, as was done at the expense of the day laborer who was displaced by the machine, the laborer was left in misery.

Then, at the precise moment when the economy needs to accelerate consumption in order to continue living, consumption refuses to walk. The reason is clear: consumption has been made the last thing in the economic process, when it belongs to the first place.

THE FAIR PRICE

The modern economy is stopped. The modern economy must come to a stop by the very logic of its "inverted" essence.

What could be done to make this economy work? The answer is very simple: re-impose the just price, of which Aristotle and Saint Thomas speak, on all things. This is the fair price, which is found in an orderly economic regime, where there is fair competition and where the price is determined by the law of supply and demand. This law is very different from the law that liberalism knew and applied. In reality, by destroying the corporate regime, eminently bourgeois liberalism unfairly applied the law of supply and demand in the price of wages, to the detriment of the worker, who received starvation wages, and in the price of the merchandise, to the detriment of the consumer, who paid for a bad and expensive item.

Now then:

> The fair price or exchange value of a thing computed in currency depends on the set of available objects, the set of resources, and the set of wills to buy and sell found in a given market. Or, if you prefer to state it as the law of supply and demand: in a market, the more considerable the quantities offered by sellers, other things being equal, prices will be lower. The smaller the quantities supplied, the higher the prices. The larger the quantities ordered by buyers, the higher the prices. The smaller the quantities ordered, the lower the prices.[16]

At present, thanks to the phenomenon of overproduction, the supply tends to infinity and demand, due to unemployment, tends to zero, and thus the just price must tend to zero. The fair price of raw materials and manufactured goods for current use must be almost zero.

This solution coincides exactly with the one we proposed in the second chapter when affirming the need for a fairer distribution of goods, as revealed by the enormous stored stocks, on the one hand, and, on the other, that enormous mass of people in misery, because their only available capital, labor, is not required.

Therefore, if the riches are stored and wasted because there is a superabundance, their value is equal to zero. If work is not required and huge masses of people wander in unemployment, it is because the work is worth zero.

Thus justice demands a pure and simple change. Zero for zero. Things should almost be given away.

The right of property cannot be invoked against this doctrine. This is because property, as we explained in the second chapter, is conditioned by the common destination of

---

16 Valére Fallon, *Economie Sociale.*

wealth to the entire human race, to common men and women. It is a necessary means, but a means, to ensure this end, that is: that no one is deprived of what they need to live. If this primary right is harmed, justice is doubtful as its foundation disappears. Likewise, then the state can intervene for a new distribution of goods, or at least, to enforce the fair price.

This is a simple and fair solution, but a fanciful one, because it would entail the bankruptcy of all financial, commercial, and industrial companies. The sale price would have to be much lower than the production price. Imagine that economic catastrophe.

However, this is an unavoidable measure, a measure that man must impose on himself, through spirit of penance. Remember the words of the Pope, in his *Caritate Christi Compulsi*, when he affirms that only prayer and penance can restore lost peace to the world:

> But to create this atmosphere of lasting peace, neither peace treaties, nor the most solemn pacts, nor international meetings or conferences, nor even the noblest and most disinterested efforts of any statesman, will be enough, unless in the first place are recognized the sacred rights of natural and divine law. No leader in public economy, no power of organization will ever be able to bring social conditions to a peaceful solution, unless first in the very field of economics there triumphs moral law based on God and conscience.[17]

This is a moral law that only prayer and penance will currently impose on the world because prayer and penance will dispel and repair the first and main cause of all rebellion and all revolution, that is, rebellion against God. This is a

17 Pius XI, "Caritate Christi Compulsi" (Encyclical, Rome, May 3, 1932).

measure that if man resists imposing it, he will impose, rather, the terrible, inflexible logic of his very economic reality.

Do not be fooled about the economic situation; it is terribly desperate. The Pope says that from the flood onwards, a spiritual and material malaise as deep and as universal as this has hardly been seen.

If the illness is serious, it needs serious and painful remedies. Let us therefore balance consumption with production and resort to the only solution, which is painful, but the only one possible.

The moment is unique in the world. The same peoples, says the Pope, are called to make a definitive choice: either they surrender to these benevolent and beneficent spiritual forces (prayer and penance) and become humble and contrite before their Lord, Father of mercy; or they abandon themselves, with the little bit of happiness still left of on earth, into the power of the enemy of God, namely, the spirit of vengeance and destruction.

Hence the ultimate solution to remedy this catastrophic result of the "inverted" economy is a spiritual solution. This is not surprising because the disease which gnaws at it is also spiritual; it is the sin of avarice, which injects the individualism of the modern world that emerged from the Reformation as its own law.

In short: economic production is ordered to consumption; consumption is ordered to man's material life; his material life to his spiritual life; and this to God. All things must be to the measure of man and man to the measure of God.

Man is the center of the earth and God is the center of the entire universe. The angels praise Him in heaven, men must serve Him on earth, and the demons tremble before Him with horror in hell.

Chapter 6

The Economic-Social Order

THUS FAR WE have studied the internal structure of the various economic values (the production of the land, industrial production with its elements of labor and capital, finance, consumption). We have also outlined the hierarchical ordering of all these values in the whole of the economy.

We said that consumption should be the proximate measure of the economy, that is, all economic values should tend and be ordered towards consumption. Things are to be produced for consumption; things must be traded to ensure a more abundant and equitable consumption; currency and its investment in capital must be used for consumption. In turn, consumption will be measured by the material demands of man, according to the condition of each one; using the words of the Angelic Doctor, we will say *that man must seek with measure the possession of external riches insofar as they are necessary to his life according to his social condition.*[a]

---

a The citation is unclear.

In short, the measure of everything is man, just as man is measured by God. God is at the pinnacle of the entire human order, because man needs to reach him in charity that culminates in the contemplation of the saints. However, for this he must order his whole life of internal operations by the practice of moral virtues. In the order of his spirit, the measure of man is the Good without measure. He must reach out to God *with all his heart, with all his soul, with all his mind, and with all his strength* (Mk 12:30). In this order, the perspectives of progress are infinite, because his spirit tends to God, who is the Infinite Good.

Yet God, who, by a design of His mercy, has constituted Himself as the measure without measure of man, does not destroy the human order; on the contrary, He requires it as a foundation that can support the infinite projections of the Divine Good. Thus the economy, destined to serve man, keeps all its reality as a humble instrument that provides man with his material bread so that he is thus able to eat spiritual bread.

It is an admirable hierarchy of values that, by restoring each reality to its own function, protects the lower ones with the support of the higher ones.

On the contrary, the modern economy that inverts all economic and human values, making infinite profit the proper object of both the economy and of all human life, destroys man and the economy, after having injured the sacred rights of God. I believe I have demonstrated this in the preceding chapters.

For this, it is necessary to uproot the profit of the economy. Yet, since profit is a perverse instinct that will always exist in the common man, it is necessary at the very least not to glorify it, not to make it the norm of life, not to make it the very engine of the economic regime. If there is profit, let it be a vicious tendency of an individual and not as a normal tendency required by the very notion of the economy itself.

On the contrary, a truly human economic regime must be structured in such a way that, taking into account the perverse instincts that nest in the heart of man, it prevents them and, as far as possible, stops them. The values of an economic construction must be exercises of virtues and not practice of vices. Hence, all the effort to demonstrate in this book the conditions under which property, capital, wages, the use of machines, and so on, can and should be integrated into a Catholic economy (the only truly economic one). For here it also follows that, in demonstrating the essential perversity of the economic regime commonly called capitalism, this book did not insist so much on criticisms that may seem typical of the men of capitalism, but on those that reveal an essentially vicious setup of the regime itself.

In short: both capitalism and socialism imply a perverse understanding of the economy, because both one and the other is the establishment in the form of a system of the disastrous vice of avarice.

This vice nested in both systems will reveal to us, in this chapter, the individualism or liberalism of capitalism; the class struggle with the proletarian glorification of socialism; from which it will result, as a conclusion, that only the corporate regime proposed by the Church can ensure an economy exorcised from profit and which is, therefore, truly human.

LIBERALISM

As with all vicious instincts, greed is egotistical. It glorifies a tendency of the *individual*; of the individual, I say and not of the man, to underline the material aspect, that is, it is something sought by the quantitative matter, true of every vicious instinct. If it is a tendency of the individual, it is material; if material, it tends to dispersion, to disintegration, to the untying of ties that unite and protect.

Hence, capitalism is a regime of untying, of dispersion, of individuals who are disintegrated like atoms and who surrender to unbridled competition.

That's why the French Revolution, which gives an official birth to capitalism, after decreeing on October 3, 1789 in the National Assembly that it will be possible "hereinafter to lend money at a fixed term with interest stipulation," promulgates on June 17, 1791 the famous "Le Chapelier" law, by which all guilds are abolished and all citizens are prohibited from re-establishing them in the future in defense of their *alleged common interests.*[b]

Article 4 of that law states[c]:

> It is contrary to the principles of liberty and the Constitution for citizens with the same professions, arts, or trades to deliberate or make agreements among themselves designed to set prices for their industry or their labor. If such deliberations and agreements are concluded, whether accompanied by oath or not, they will be declared unconstitutional, prejudicial to liberty and the Declaration of the Rights of Man, and will be null and void.

Here, in the name of the Rights of Man, the freedom to associate has been forbidden. Behold that man is condemned to be a mere individual in the infinite dispersion of millions of other individuals. All individuals, untied from the ties that protect, are delivered up to free competition.

Pure freedom (or the untying of bonds) has been erected as a system: freedom of trade and exchange; freedom of work for men, women, and children; absolute freedom to contract working conditions; unlimited freedom to possess; the

b The Le Chapelier Law (14 June 1791): "Article 1. In that the abolition of any kind of citizen's guild in the same trade or of the same profession is one of the fundamental bases of the French Constitution, it is forbidden to reestablish them under any pretext or in any form whatsoever."

c Meinvielle cites article 3.

prohibition of all labor regulations regarding the minimum wage, the duration of the day, the hygienic conditions of the workshop.

Individuals remain unarmed among themselves, under the surveillance of the state, whose mission is reduced, like that of the traffic agent, to guaranteeing individual freedom. What is the immediate fate of this economic regime? It will be exactly the same as a garden of tame and ferocious animals, in which the walls that separate some species from others have suddenly been demolished. What must necessarily happen? The weak, in the clutches of the strong, will be eliminated or reduced to ominous servitude, while the strong will exercise outright domination. This is because the strong, favored by their arrogance, will gradually deprive the weak of resources and increase their power in proportion to their weakening, until imposing, in the words of Leo XIII, on the *innumerable multitude* of proletarians a yoke which differs little from that of the slaves.[d]

The history of capitalism in its two stages of free competition and economic dictatorship, has been wonderfully traced by Pope Pius XI in *Quadragesimo Anno*, when he writes:

> In the first place, it is obvious that not only is wealth concentrated in our times but an immense power and despotic economic dictatorship is consolidated in the hands of a few. . . . This concentration of power and might, the characteristic mark, as it were, of contemporary economic life, is the fruit that the unlimited freedom of struggle among competitors has of its own nature produced, and which lets only the strongest survive; and this is often the same as saying, those who fight the most violently, those

d Leo XIII, "Rerum Novarum," 3.

> who give least heed to their conscience. . . . Free competition has destroyed itself; economic dictatorship has supplanted the free market; unbridled ambition for power has likewise succeeded greed for gain; all economic life has become tragically hard, inexorable, and cruel.[e]

Economic liberalism is essentially a bourgeois despotism in the same way that complete freedom in a garden of animals is the reign of the tiger. Under the pretext of the rights of man, the French Revolution has promulgated the domination of the individual-bourgeois, of the man-stomach, who since that day has enslaved spiritual values with the subjection of the Church to the State, intellectual values with the servitude of intelligence to technology, moral values with the secularization of life, political values with the stupid myth of popular sovereignty, and economic values with harsh slavery for the worker.

SOCIALISM

How long will the bourgeois dictatorship that we are enduring last? It is not easy to know, but it seems the time is near when he makes room for his despotic half-brother, socialism, who burns with envious desire to supplant him.

In fact, socialism is nothing more than the same vice of avarice projected into the hearts of those who have nothing, just as liberalism is avarice in the hearts of those who have. It is the glorification or systematization of the envy of wealth. It is a *sadness*, as Saint Thomas says, because of the goods which the bourgeois possesses in abundance.[1] For this reason, the current economic society can be broken down into liberals and

1 ST II-II, q. 36, a. 2.

e Pius XI, "Quadragesimo Anno," 105, 107, 109.

socialists, that is, into the greed of those who have and the greed of those who do not have.

For this reason socialism should be considered in two stages: in the stage of ascension (preferably, social democracy or parliamentary socialism), in its struggle to seize the bourgeois trenches with its decanted program of workers' demands, and in the state of attainment, with the realization of the proletarian paradise (Soviet communism).

In the first stage socialism is loquacious, flattering, and opportunistic. It is a terrible enemy of the bourgeois understanding of life and is the indomitable coryphaeus of the violated rights of the worker.

This is in general, because if a socialist, even at this stage, is given a decent ascension into bourgeois society, all his phobias disappear as if by magic.

In the second stage, when a definitive socialist domination has been achieved with the crushing of the bourgeoisie, socialism is a super-capitalism that has changed masters. Having cast off the bourgeoisie, it is replaced by an oligarchy composed partly of professionals and partly of proletarians, and the economic society essentially continues with the same configuration that it had in economic liberalism.

The old traces of capitalism, weakly outlined by the logic of economic liberalism, are now underlined and erected into law by socialism.

If in capitalism human society appears divided into two great classes, of which one in misery works for the benefit of the other who has accumulated wealth, the same division appears in socialism or communism: on the one hand, there is the State in the hands of a few, the only capitalist who usurps 70 percent of the workers' wages, as is currently the case in Russia; and on the other hand an immense starving multitude, condemned to servitude by decree of law.

Class struggle belongs to the essence of economic liberalism and socialism, because as one and the other are mixed with greed, and greed accumulates for itself to the detriment of others or envy at what others possess with the desire to take it, one and the other imply an eternal struggle between the possessors. Class struggle exists in liberalism by the logic of free competition, and in socialism as the imposition of the proletarian program.

CATHOLIC DOCTRINE REGARDING THE HUMAN PERSON

Only Catholicism, which has a doctrine received from God, can transcend this domain of vicious instincts that divide some men against others and understands that, despite the coverings and appearances that diversify men, all are equally human persons, regenerated by the blood of Christ and destined to see the Divine Essence. "There is neither Jew nor Greek, there is neither slave nor free person, there is not male and female; for you are all one in Christ Jesus,"[f] said the Apostle Saint Paul. On the other hand, if the Divine Essence is the wealth reserved for every man, it is not necessary to worry about what we will eat, what we will drink, or how we will dress.[2]

Economic concern occupies a very secondary place among human concerns. The wealth of this world is not more valuable than poverty; On the contrary, poverty has been declared *blessed* by the One who sanctified and exalted it in its nakedness in the manger and on Calvary, while wealth has been called wicked.[3] The rich man, if he does not want to hear the curse of Jesus Christ who said, "Woe to you who are rich. . . . it is easier for a camel to pass through the eye of a needle than for one who is rich to enter the kingdom of God," if you do not want to hear this curse, you must detach your heart from the

2 Mt 6:25-34.
3 Lk 16:9.

f Gal 3:28.

possession of wealth and use what God has granted you in the humble service of the poor.[g]

The only wealth of the Christian is the Poverty of Jesus Christ. For this reason, the first converts to the Faith, the believers, "All who believed were together and had all things in common; they would sell their property and possessions and divide them among all according to each one's need."[4]

It is necessary to deduce from this, not the stupid and utopian implantation of a communist regime, but that, after the manifestation of Jesus Christ to the world, "there is need of only one thing," [Lk 10:42] in the face of which neither poverty nor wealth matter, so that the avarice of the rich man who accumulates to the detriment of the poor is as perverse and foolish as the avarice of the poor man who burns with the desire to seize the wealth of the rich.[5] "Take care," said Christ, "to guard against all greed, for though one may be rich, one's life does not consist of possessions."[6]

It is necessary to understand, above all, that the diversity of the natural social conditions and of fortunes is something entirely secondary in the face of the dignity of the human person called to participate in the Divine Vision.

THE NEED FOR SOCIAL FUNCTIONS

Nevertheless, this diversity of conditions, be they natural, social, and of fortunes is necessary and fitting, and therefore desired by God. As Leo XIII says:

> There naturally exist among mankind manifold differences of the most important kind; people differ in capacity, skill, health, strength; and

4 Acts 2:44-45; Meinvielle gives only v. 44.
5 Lk 10:42.
6 Lk 12:15; Meinvielle erroneously gives 10:15.

g Lk 6:24; Mt 19:24.

> unequal fortune is a necessary result of unequal condition. Such unequality is far from being disadvantageous either to individuals or to the community. Social and public life can only be maintained by means of various kinds of capacity for business and the playing of many parts; and each man, as a rule, chooses the part which suits his own peculiar domestic condition. . . . The great mistake made in regard to the matter now under consideration is to take up with the notion that class is naturally hostile to class, and that the wealthy and the working men are intended by nature to live in mutual conflict. So irrational and so false is this view that the direct contrary is the truth. Just as the symmetry of the human frame is the result of the suitable arrangement of the different parts of the body, so in a State is it ordained by nature that these two classes should dwell in harmony and agreement, so as to maintain the balance of the body politic.[7]

Let us remember that nature demands diversity of different orders set in a hierarchy according to the dignity of the functions: the priestly order, which cares for spiritual interests; the political order, which is reserved for the earthly destiny of human societies; the military order, which places itself at the service of the earthly community to defend it against possible external disturbances; the intellectual and artistic order, which places immense intellectual riches at the service of the human community; the economic order, which seeks what is necessary for human well-being for the benefit of the whole society.

In the economic order itself, there must be a diversity of functions according to the diversity of domains, such as the

7 Leo XIII, "Rerum Novarum," 17, 19.

production of the land and of industry, commerce and finance; within each realm, there must be different tasks for the boss and the worker, for the master and the servant, for the manager and the employee.

To understand the Catholic understanding of social and economic life it is necessary to admit all the various functions from the lowest to the highest and to accept the hierarchical subordination of one to another. The priestly order is superior to the political order, and the political superior to the economic one. Nonetheless, all three are equally necessary, just as their hierarchical subordination is necessary for the just existence of all three. If the political order supplants the priestly one, politics is weakened and vulnerable to being supplanted by the economic one. Thus, the royal power that rebelled against the priesthood, when Philip the Fair rose up against Boniface VIII in the twelfth century, was reduced to servitude by economic power with the French Revolution. Now, economic power will be destroyed by the proletarian revolution.

LABOR UNIONS

What I will say is common doctrine of the Church, taught especially in Leo XIII's *Rerum Novarum* and in Pius XI's *Quadragesimo anno*.

First of all, against liberalism and socialism, let us recall the sacred right and obligation that belongs to every man, even independently of the State, to build associations with which he defends his legitimate interests. As Leo XIII says, "To enter into a 'society' of this kind is the natural right of man; and the State has for its office to protect natural rights, not to destroy them."[h]

Furthermore, man should not find himself unarmed in front of another man as liberalism claims, nor in front of the

h Leo XIII, 51.

State as socialism wants, because in both cases man would be forced into slavery. It is therefore necessary to restore, adapting them to the needs of the present time,[i] "that rich social life which was once highly developed through associations of various kinds."[j]

We can reduce to three the economic-social groups that must be established in an economy to obtain, in the current material conditions (I say matter as opposed to form, as I explained in the first chapter) a Christian ordering of economic life: unions properly speaking, the organization of the professions, and interprofessional organizations.

Unions are formed freely within the organized profession that harmonizes the rights of the employer and the worker. The unions will therefore be workers' unions and employers' unions.

Obviously, the ones that above all represent a special interest are the workers' unions, because the worker (the same can be said of any employee) is in conditions of inferiority with respect to the boss; he therefore needs to use the union with his co-workers to enforce his rights. However, the employers' union is also necessary, either as a prior condition to the organization of the professions, and above all to standardize the treatment due to the workers in all the establishments of the same industry. In practice, Christian employers' unions are more difficult to establish than workers' unions.

The Church currently greatly encourages priests and laity to hasten, above all, the creation of openly Christian labor unions, that is, trade unions that effectively ensure the rights of workers of one same profession or industry with regard to salary, duration and conditions for work, the development of professional education, the regulation of apprenticeship,

i Cf. Leo XIII, "Rerum Novarum."

j Pius XI, "Quadragesimo Anno," 78.

insurance against unemployment and work accidents, the effectiveness of legitimate strikes, and so on.

Very well-known today is the sentence of the Sacred Congregation of the Council, pronounced on June 25, 1929 and addressed to the Bishop of Lila, in which said Congregation resolved a conflict that arose between industrialists and workers of that region and at the same time established the doctrine of the Church on labor unionization.[k]

1. The Church recognizes and affirms the right of employers and workers to form trade union associations, whether separate or mixed, and sees in them an effective means of resolving the social question.
2. In the current circumstances, the Church considers the establishment of such trade union associations to be morally necessary.
3. The Church urges the establishment of such trade union associations.
4. The Church wants trade union associations to be established and governed according to the principles of the Christian faith and morals.
5. The Church wants trade union associations to be instruments of harmony and peace, and to this end suggests the constitution of mixed commissions as a means of union between them.
6. The Church wants trade union associations created by Catholics for Catholics to be formed among Catholics, without ignoring, however, that particular needs may force groups to proceed in a different way.
7. The Church recommends the union of Catholics for a common work with the bonds of Christian charity.

It is not possible to express the Church's will more energetically, a will which urgently wants Catholic

k Despite Meinvielle's insistence, the document is practically unknown and untraceable today.

unionization. We should not admire this imperious will. The Church is a Mother, and she is seriously concerned about the fate of millions and millions of her children, workers who turn to socialism, communism, and trade unionism, with the evident danger to their baptized souls, because they believe that there they will find the defense of their legitimate rights as workers.

It is therefore necessary to promote the unionization of Catholic workers to ensure the spiritual and material welfare of the worker. The responsibility incumbent on Catholic priests and laity is very serious. Remaining indifferent to the loss of so many souls that the Lord loves, souls who are lost due to the negligence of Catholics, is a grave sin of omission. If in times of the Christian faith, Catholics moved by charity dedicated themselves to rescuing captives, today it is necessary to do exactly the same. The slavery of the worker, either by bourgeois oppression or by proletarian oppression, is evident. Hence, the workers must be redeemed. Charity and social justice demand it. In the Christian nations of Europe, work is being carried out with considerable fruit in this crusade for the dignity of the workers. The *International Christian Trade Union* has a large contingent of 3,000,000 adherents.

Among us almost nothing has been done.[1] However, it is something seriously required by charity and social justice, as the Supreme Pontiffs teach. In addition, whatever is done for the Christian education of the worker is almost completely useless as long as there is no Christian atmosphere in the union setting.

CORPORATIVE REGIME

On the other hand, the Church strongly recommends the formation of trade unions as a step towards the definitive

1 Presumably Meinvielle is referring to Argentina.

reorganization of Christian society, which will need to be made concrete with the legal organization of the professions, or, to express myself in the classic language of the socially involved Catholics of France, with the *régime corporatif*.

According to the definition given by the Freiburg Union:

> The corporative regime is the mode of social organization based on the grouping of men according to the community of their natural interests and their social function, and by necessary crowning the public and distinct representation of these different organisms.

Pius XI proclaims the need for this organization of professional life to resurface:

> When we speak of the reform of institutions, the State comes chiefly to mind, not as if universal well-being were to be expected from its activity, but because things have come to such a pass through the evil of what we have termed 'individualism' that, following upon the overthrow and near extinction of that rich social life which was once highly developed through associations of various kinds, there remain virtually only individuals and the State. This is to the great harm of the State itself; for, with a structure of social governance lost, and with the taking over of all the burdens which the wrecked associations once bore. the State has been overwhelmed and crushed by almost infinite tasks and duties.[8]

8 Pius XI, "Quadragesimo Anno," 78.

PROFESSIONAL ORGANIZATION

Once the formation of different and independent trade union groups (workers' unions and employers' unions in the same industry or profession) has been accomplished, these should be grouped together in the professional body. A mixed committee, composed of an equal number of delegates from the two groups (employers and workers), will exercise, with legal recognition, the governance of the profession. It will determine the general mandatory working conditions for all members of the profession, whether business owners, employees, or workers. It will also assure compliance with these conditions through specially designated inspectors, issues judgments in the case of infractions, will prevent conflicts between employers and workers, and will manage corporate assets.

Although they receive authority through their legal recognition, the establishment of these professional bodies as social bodies is required by the Church's social doctrine as Pius XI explains in *Quadragesimo Anno*. After noting:

> as the situation now stands, hiring and offering for hire in the so-called labor market separate men into two divisions, as into battle lines, and the contest between these divisions turns the labor market itself almost into a battlefield where, face to face, the opposing lines struggle bitterly. Everyone understands that this grave evil which is plunging all human society to destruction must be remedied as soon as possible. But complete cure will not come until this opposition has been abolished and well-ordered members of the social body - Industries and Professions - are constituted in which men may have their place, not according to the position each has in the labor market but according to the respective social

> functions which each performs. For under nature's guidance it comes to pass that just as those who are joined together by nearness of habitation establish towns, so those who follow the same industry or profession - whether in the economic or other field - form guilds or associations, so that many are wont to consider these self-governing organizations, if not essential, at least natural to civil society.[9]

INTERPROFESSIONAL ORGANIZATION

Once the different professions have been organized, it will be necessary to organize them all, as a whole, according to the hierarchy of their respective purposes within the national character of production. This is the interprofessional organization that Pius XI also speaks of. For this, a directive body of the entire national economy will be constituted, made up of delegates from the different organized professions (employers, technicians, employees, workers), in all domains of agricultural, livestock, industrial, commercial, and financial production, so that a true socio-economic organism can be established in this way to which the Apostle's words about the mystical Body of Christ can be applied, says the Pope: "the whole body, joined and held together by every supporting ligament, with the proper functioning of each part, brings about the body's growth and builds itself up in love."[m]

Economic activity, whose essential order we have outlined in the preceding chapters, will thus achieve an effective ordering. Consumption will be the great law of the economy. The production of the land will recover its primary function with a rural and domestic physiognomy. Industrial production

9 Pius XI, "Quadragesimo Anno," 83.

m Eph 4:16.

will follow, where, in addition to the large company, the rehabilitated crafts will have a powerful boost. Commercial professions and stable organizations for the financing of production will come later; these organisms will no longer be founded upon loans at interest, which will be resolutely banished, but on the basis of capitals that will be risked in production, with the consequent advantages and disadvantages.

In this way, the economic regime thus brought about will not be capitalism emptied into corporations (the utopia that many unconsciously promote) but a new economic order, from which greed has truly been banished; and that if men act out of avarice, it is not by virtue of the economic order, but in a certain way opposed to it.

Yet, for the effectiveness and stability of such a regime it is in no way fitting for individuals to feel restricted or violated. A soul must give life to this body. The idea that we all form a body with a common interest must penetrate into everyone's consciousness as the impulse of economic life. Life is not a struggle of one class against another, as liberalism and socialism have supposed, but rather a collaboration. There must be collaboration within a company, for a better and more equitable performance, as well as collaboration within the same profession, to avoid unfair or disastrous competition; there must be interprofessional collaboration, to realize the greatness of a useful national production, as well as collaboration in the international order, because "since the various nations largely depend on one another in economic matters and need one another's help, they should strive with a united purpose and effort to promote by wisely conceived pacts and institutions a prosperous and happy international cooperation in economic life."[10]

10 Pius XI, "Quadragesimo Anno," 89.

THE STATE AND CORPORATE REGIME

With the rights of all individuals secured in this way, that is, by means of trade unions and professional and interprofessional associations, the country's economic interests are likewise assured. Together with this, its other cultural, intellectual interests, and the like in the hierarchy of their respective goals are also assured, and hence it is possible to establish the tasks that are proper to the state. The State is the one who directs the *common good.* Hence, it must be concerned with "directing, watching, urging, restraining, as occasion requires and necessity demands,"[11] the whole social body. However, it must not replace the body's activities. It should not absorb it but protect it, having understood, as Pius XI says, that "those in power should be sure that the more perfectly a graduated order is kept among the various associations, in observance of the principle of 'subsidiary function,' the stronger social authority and effectiveness will be the happier and more prosperous the condition of the State."[12]

Economic activity must not be confused with political activity. Political authority effectively directs the pre-existing social forces, and among them the economic ones, directing them towards the common good. Hence, it presupposes the existence of social activities that have their own constitution and movement. The economic activity organized in the corporative regime is thus outside of the State, although under its political regulation.

The purely social, as opposed to statuary, character of corporations must be resolutely emphasized. Corporations must have a life of their own, not a life borrowed from a higher power.

11 Pius XI, 80.

12 Pius XI, 80.

In this sense, it must be acknowledged that the experiences of *Corporatism* carried out by Italy, Austria, Portugal and Germany have not yet achieved their own value. If they cannot guarantee surviving the ever-present possibility of a national crisis, these groups cannot be considered entrenched. They turn out to be merely artificial creations.

ESTABLISHMENT OF THE CORPORATE REGIME

This does not mean that knowing the efforts of these nations to straighten the economy is the only legitimate path. However, neither should we be easily deluded by the emergence of these experiences, just as we should not be discouraged if they fail.

The great difficulty that remains is to figure out how the establishment of a corporative regime would be possible. Should the State establish it from above, as something done, or rather should it be prepared from below, as a requirement of economic life itself that calls for it?

The action from above that establishes and that from below that prepares are indispensable, because if everything comes from above, it will be an artificial creation without roots; if it is expected to come from below, it is vain to wait for it to break through the environment saturated with greed, which, by definition, is contrary to the collaboration of the *Corporate Regime*.

The State must impose it, but first the demand for its imposition must be felt within the conscience of the masses.

Perhaps this demand will make itself felt in a truly perceptible way in the presently numb consciences of the economic masses, when the point of chaos is at its height and the intended untried solutions have been exhausted. A leader of peoples might then arise, a leader whom Providence sends in the most desperate moments, and the Corporate Regime will remain rooted for the health and economic well-being of the people.

INTERNATIONAL ECONOMIC COLLABORATION

Only once the national economy and life have been secured, through an autonomous vital functioning under the State's energetic protection, can there be thoughts of organizing international economic activity. The international organization of the economy will not only attenuate the dangers of competition, but will also divide the work and coordinate the activities according to the economic possibilities of each people. Hence, Pius XI says, "since the various nations largely depend on one another in economic matters and need one another's help, they should strive with a united purpose and effort to promote by wisely conceived pacts and institutions a prosperous and happy international cooperation in economic life."[13]

I have had to outline in broad strokes the configuration of the economic edifice in accord with the Church's doctrine. After this exposition, it is worth asking: how far is it possible to carry out this outline? What is the fate of this unbridled economy that we are suffering? There are so many other questions that would require a long and detailed answer.

However, from the metaphysical, theological point of view, from which we have positioned ourselves to judge economic phenomena and determine their just and beneficial conformation, it will be relatively easy to ascertain an answer.

In short: if we look closely at the current rhythm of life and especially that of the economy, we see that everything boils down to an "inversion of values," to the "fortuitous expansion of certain individualities," to "a mad urge to run, for acceleration," to "a frightful domination of profit, of greed."

In reality, these are different aspects of the same phenomenon, because greed, which is infinite, causes acceleration, and this, in turn, the expansion of certain individualities over others; with all this comes an evident

13 Pius XI, "Quadragesimo Anno," 80.

inversion of values, so that what should dominate and maintain the balance of the lower realities is crushed under the anarchy of these same realities.

At the moment, the Church does not and cannot have even the slightest chance, not of imposing, but of making people (even the majority of her Catholic children) understand what are the demands of a Christian and human life and economy. Why? As long as the rhythm of life that I have just indicated continues, the Church, which is the Spiritual Reality itself, which therefore implies sitting at the pinnacle of all realizable values here on the earthly plan, the one that keeps them all in their just balance, will be crushed, indeed, smothered, under the anarchy of all other realities that have risen up in rebellion.

How long will this anarchy last? Until it reaches its culmination, as I have said many times and will repeat it once more. The world has been in a process of degradation for more than 400 years. This entire process of decomposition, indicated by Luther, Descartes, and Rousseau as its most visible milestones, is reflected in the French Revolution, which is the revolution par excellence: the Revolution against God, against His Christ, and against the Church. Yet the French Revolution is not the end but rather the birth of a new world, in which the rights of Man are proclaimed in opposition to the rights of God. This new world is essentially economic, because either God is served, or Mammon is served, which is the idol of Wealth. The world of the French Revolution did not want to serve God, so it must necessarily worship Mammon.

In the economic world, however, there is the boss and the worker, the bourgeois and the proletarian, liberalism and socialism. The boss, the bourgeois, and liberalism have already dominated, and now—precisely when it was thought that they had reached the zenith of their careers—they find themselves weakened and disoriented, while their irreconcilable step-brother, socialism, feels strong and with an ambition to dominate: the Proletarian revolution seems to me imminent throughout the world. These next 10 or 20 years will be full of terrible surprises. Desperate, man will get fed up with his brother's blood. Glorified by the French Revolution, humanity will finish off the last remains of barbarism; it will be something much more frightful than the attack of the barbarians on the Roman Empire.

And the Church? The Church will need to restore the meaning of life to this desperate humanity, giving a Christian education to these new barbarians.

Chapter 7

Epilogue

If it were possible to order the economy without ordering life, this book could already be shut. However, while the economy is a concern in life, it is not the only one. What place does it occupy in life? Consider a civilization placed exclusively under the economy: what characteristics should it have, at what moment should it arise, how does it begin, and where must it end?

Here are so many other questions that require a mind that reads. This answer comes from these reflections on the current situation on the occasion of the Encyclical *Caritate Christi Compulsi* that Pope Pius XI addressed to the world, commenting on this crisis of Capitalism.[1]

It is not my intent here to comment on this Encyclical; I only want to outline some reflections on what, in my opinion, constitutes the central theme of it, that is, the serious difficulty that the world is going through today. The Pope writes:

> In this state of things, Venerable Brethren, stirred up by the selfsame charity of Christ, We once more address you all, and the faithful committed

1 From 1932.

> to your care, and indeed all men, exhorting all and several that with all their forces united in a spirit of charity they should endeavor to withstand, by every possible effort, the calamities by which civil society is now afflicted and those yet graver calamities threatening it in the future.[a]

Hence, in the Pope's thought, the current situation has a very special significance: not simply because it is current, that is, because it has become present to us (so great is the fatuity of the modern individual that he imagines himself to be the axis of the universe through time and space), but because in reality the existence of humanity itself will be determined here and now. If humanity does not want to be plunged into a frightful chaos (as the Pontiff says: if it wants to be free from the danger of terror or anarchy), it must find security in the present moment.

The present moment is decisive, critical for the very roots of humanity. Just as humanity succumbed in one catastrophe, in the flood, in the same way it seems that it is about to succumb in another:

> Anyone who considers carefully the prolonged and bitter series of sufferings, the unhappy heritage of sin, whereby, as by so many stages, we mark the course of fallen man in this mortal pilgrimage, can hardly find any occasion since the flood, when the race of man was so deeply and so commonly tried by so many and such great distresses of body and of mind as those which we lament to see in the present troubles.[b]

This very profound importance of the present moment explains why it is the object of singular predictions both in the

a Pius XI, "Caritate Christi Compulsi," 1.

b Pius XI, 2.

traditional books of all peoples as well as in the prophetic spirit of the saints. This moment, then, takes on a singularly privileged significance, and this not so much because it marks the passage from one culture to another, but rather from culture itself to a lack of culture, to chaos. What is the current moment, considered from a cultural standpoint?

In order to weigh the cultural density at any historical moment, it is necessary to consider it in terms of the past and the future. Every historical moment is a link in an essentially movable chain. Only the past and the future can reveal to us whether a point is progress or regress, and to what extent.

The current moment is one of very deep cultural regression, of immediate regression to death. I will limit myself to the consideration, in this regard, of Christian culture, that is, of the culture of the European continent that has been under the influence of Christian action.

If, in my hypothesis, the current moment is one of regression, it will be necessary to indicate the culminating point from which we are moving away.

The fullness of the cultural ascension was achieved in a visible way—within the inevitable imperfection of fallen humanity—in the thirteenth century, when the social action of Christianity was represented by Popes Innocent IV and Saint Gregory X and by Saint Louis King of France; when its intellectual activity was illuminated with the intelligence of Saint Bonaventure and Saint Thomas Aquinas; when artistic activity shone in the frescoes of Blessed Fra Angelico, in Dante's *Divine Comedy*, and in Chartres Cathedral; and when, above all these works of the human spirit that have never been surpassed, it remains so empty of itself that it does not manage to exclaim, except with Saint Thomas Aquinas to his confrere Reginald who encouraged him to continue the *Summa Theologica*: "Reginaldo, non possum; omnia que scripsi vídentur mihi palea" [Reginald, I cannot; everything that I have written seems like straw to me."].

Why was this a high point of human culture?

This was a high point because that period of history marks, in a particular culture, the culminating point to which the human spirit can reach in the essential things. Note that I say that this is a culminating point and not the only possible one. Note above all that I call it culminating because in it "the essential perfection of man" has been achieved, and with this I indicate the criterion that should guide us in the appreciation of cultures. A culture is nothing more than "man manifesting himself."

A culture will be all the richer the richer man's manifestations. The value of these manifestations must be weighed according to their content of reality. The Subsistent Reality is God, from whom all good derives and of whom all finite good is but a participation. Hence, a culture will be all the richer the "more divine, the closer to God" the manifestations of man are.

Man, who is a conflict of pure potency and pure act, can realize cultures as diverse as the divine culture of the Middle Ages and the diabolical one of Communist Russia.

Man is a conflict of "pure potency and pure act." He is "pure potency" because, as Aristotle and Saint Thomas explain, the human intellect is in potency with respect to all intelligibles, and for this reason, at the beginning man is like a *tabula rasa* in which there is nothing written. He is "pure act" because, thanks to the activity of the agent intellect, everything intelligible can be actualized. Hence man can rise from the lowest reality to God by participation, or he can be content with being only a man as happened in the rationalism of the classical age, or he can become an animal as happens with the man of the nineteenth century, or he can simply be "chaos" as the proletarian dictatorship insists on forging man.

Since the Redemption, in man, that conflict of pure potency and pure act, four fundamental formalities coexist, four formalities that explain the four possible stages of a cultural heaven.

Indeed: man is something: he is a being.

Man is an animal: he is a sensitive, delightful being.

The man is a man: he is a rational, honest being. Above these three formalities in the current providence, as the Creator has constituted it:

Man is god: he is called to the life proper to God.

Hence, there are four essential formalities in man:

- The supernatural or divine formality.
- The human or rational formality.
- The animal or sensitive formality.
- The formality of reality, of thing.

In a normally constituted man (let us say also in a normal culture, since the culture is man manifesting himself) these four formalities must be articulated in a hierarchical subordination that ensures the unity of his operations.

Man is a thing in order to sense like an animal; he senses like an animal in order to reason and understand like a man; he reasons and understands as a man in order to love God as God. In other words: the formality of reality that there is in him must be subordinated to his function as an animal; that of animal, to his function as man; that of man, to that of God. This is confirmed even in the experimental sciences by the fact that the physical-chemical processes of man are at the service of the vegetative functions; these, at the service of the normal functioning of the senses; the sensitive life ensures the acquisition of ideas and the superior psychological life, with the whole of the economic, political, and moral order, all of which is nothing more than a means for man to communicate with his Creator. For these reasons, Saint Thomas Aquinas was able to write the profound statement that all human occupations seem to serve those who contemplate the truth.[2]

2 SCG III, c. 37.

In other words: mysticism, the infused contemplation of the Saints, which is nothing but the highest exercise of holiness, is above all men, and just as there can be no man more human than the saint, there can be no culture more cultural (of greater cultural density) than that which is under the sign of sanctity, as it was—within the inevitable imperfection of what is human—in the medieval culture.

If these four formalities that constitute man are socially projected, there are four well-characterized functions:

- To the formality of thing corresponds the economic function of execution—work and the worker.
- The formality of the animal corresponds to the economic function of management—capital and the bourgeoisie.
- To the formality of man corresponds political functions—the aristocracy and nobility.
- To the formality of God corresponds religious functions—the priesthood.

Before indicating what is the proper scope of each of these functions, let us observe that the first three are of human right, that is, they can be realized in various forms as long as their essential nature is respected; not so the fourth, the priesthood, which, by the will of Christ, is surrounded by its concrete form of constitution in the Episcopate united with the Roman Pontiff. Indeed, Jesus Christ, the Son of God, to Whom all power in heaven and on earth have been given, has communicated His mission to the Episcopate in union with the Roman Pontiff, when in the person of Peter and the apostles He said: "Go, therefore, and make disciples of all nations, baptizing them in the name of the Father, and of the Son, and of the holy Spirit, teaching them to observe all that I have commanded you. And behold, I am with you always, until the end of the age."[c]

c Mt 28:19-20.

What are the attributions that are proper to each of these functions?

The priesthood, let us say the Church, has the task of ensuring man's divine life by incorporating him into the society of God's children and keeping him in it. For this, the Church exercises the functions of Teacher, and in this capacity she is the depositary and authentic interpreter of all the truths revealed to man by God. The Church exercises the functions of Priest, and in this capacity sanctifies all its sinful members with the power that springs from the Perennial Sacrifice. The Church exercises the function of Pastor, and in this capacity governs men's conduct.

Its domain extends to the entire spiritual realm, which can be internal and external, private and public, individual, domestic, or social. Nothing that in one way or another has relevance to the eternal order is foreign to its jurisdiction.

If a prince's temporal government harms God's glory and the eternal salvation of his subjects, the Church can and must, by virtue of its universal jurisdiction in spiritual matters, apply coercive measures against that prince, which can go as far as his deposition.

The political function is what founds the existence of the aristocracy or nobility, and has as its own goal to make human coexistence virtuous. Humans must live in society in order to achieve their human perfection. However, this society must be human because the bond of union must be proper to man. This bond of union is virtue, and the bringing about of this union is the function proper to that social class that, in one way or another, has political functions in its hands. That class can only be the aristocratic class, that is, government of the virtuous in the etymological sense, since only those who possess virtue can make it reign.

The aristocracy does not define what virtue consists of. That is the task of the priestly power. The aristocracy brings to a practical realization the state of virtue, the knowledge of which it has learned from priestly lips.

Hence the aristocracy's subordination to the priesthood is essential, just as the subordination of politics to theology is essential.

Below the aristocratic order are the lower classes, the bourgeoisie and craftsmen, dedicated to the economic function of preparing the things necessary for man's material subsistence. The bourgeoisie intervenes in financial and mercantile operations and in the management of industries; the craftsmen, in the carrying out of the different necessities of life. One leads, another executes. One contributes the capital and the other contributes his labor. Nevertheless, one and the other live associated in a spirit of mutual collaboration within the economic sphere.

The four essential functions that we have just explained, as well as the four formalities that constitute man, are joined in a hierarchy of mutual service.

The artisan serves the bourgeoisie, and the bourgeoisie serves the artisan insofar as it directs and protects it, just as vegetative life prepares the sensory organs and in turn is served by them, since the animal procures vegetative sustenance through its senses.

The craftsmanship and the bourgeoisie, united in the economic system, serve the nobility, since they ensure its economic support; in turn they are served by the nobility, since the nobility ensures the virtuous order, in the same way that the senses contribute to the acquisition of ideas and man with his ideas rectifies and perfects the sensitive knowledge.

The craftsmen, the bourgeoisie, and the nobility serve the priesthood, since the first two ensure economic support and the third, virtuous coexistence; in turn, these three are served by the priesthood since the priesthood consolidates the economic and political order with sanctifying virtue that it dispenses, in a way analogous to how man, with his understanding, is convinced of the need to accept supernatural Revelation, and supernatural Revelation in turn consolidates the knowledge of natural truths.

A normal order of life is essentially a hierarchical order, a hierarchy of services. The hierarchical order integrates the manifold into a unity. Hence families are integrated into the unity of corporations; corporations, in the unity of the nation under the same political regime; the nations in the unity of Christianity through the worship of the same God, in the same baptism and in the same Spirit.

If the normal order is hierarchy, abnormality is a violation of the hierarchy, and at the same time, a process of atomization, since, by breaking the hierarchy, the principle of unity is broken and the causes of multiplication, which induce death, are given free reign. Indeed, death is nothing more than the disintegration of the one into the many.

Which and how many types of abnormality are essentially possible?

There are three, and only three, types of abnormality, since there are three possible fundamental relations, namely:

- That the natural rebel against the supernatural, or the nobility against the priesthood, or politics against theology; here is the first rebellion.
- That the animal rebels against the natural, or the bourgeoisie against the nobility, or the economic leader against politics; here is the second rebellion.
- That something rebels against the animal, or the craftsmen against the bourgeoisie or the economic leader; here is the third rebellion.

In the first revolution, if what is political rebels against what is theological, what must come about it a culture of political expansion, of natural or rational expansion, of monarchical expression that is, at the same time, one of religious oppression.

It is precisely the culture that was inaugurated with the Renaissance and was known by the names of:

- Humanism
- Rationalism
- Naturalism
- Absolutism
- Caesaropapism

In the second revolution, if the bourgeois economic realm rebels against the political, there must be a culture of economic expansion, animal expansion, bourgeois expansion, and political oppression.

This is precisely the culture that was inaugurated with the French Revolution and that is known by the names of:

- Economism
- Capitalism
- Animalism
- The stupid century
- Democracy

In the third revolution, if the proletarian economic realm rebels against the bourgeois economic field, it will necessarily produce a culture of proletarian expansion, nihilistic expansion, and bourgeois oppression.

Again, this is precisely the culture that is inaugurated with the communist revolution and that is known with the names of:

- Communism
- War on capitalism
- Bourgeoisie war

It is the last and chaotic revolution because man does not affirm anything; rather, he turns against what exists and destroys it.

But let's not get ahead of ourselves. Let us now see, although we should return to the mentioned concepts, how this process of rebellion has been taking place since the Middle Ages until now.

The Middle Ages were essentially theocentric, theological, or priestly, because all human activities, each unfolding within its own sphere with an admirable economy, worked towards man's union with God. It was priestly because, since the priest is the visible repository of God's word, he must order a world whose longing is the visible realization of this word.

Before placing the crown on the king's head, the officiating archbishop asked the following six questions:

- "Does Your Majesty want to preserve the holy Catholic and apostolic faith and fortify it with just works?
- Does Your Majesty want to protect the Church and her servants?
- Does Your Majesty want to govern the empire that God entrusts to you according to the justice of our Fathers and promise to defend it energetically?
- Does Your Majesty want to maintain the rights of the Empire, reconquer the States that have been unjustly separated and govern them in such a way as to serve the interests of the Empire?
- Does Your Majesty want to show himself to be an equitable judge and loyal defender of the poor as well as of the rich, of widows and orphans?
- Does Your Majesty want to give the Pope and the Holy Roman Church the obedience, fidelity, and respect that are due?"

After taking the oath, the officiating archbishop turned to the assembled bodies of state, as well as to the rest of the assembly, who in the spirit of the ceremony represented the entire people, and questioning them said:

> "Do you want to strengthen his reign? Do you consent to pay him faith and homage? Do you

> undertake to submit to all his commandments according to the word of the Apostle, that each one be subject to the authority that has power over him and to the king who is the supreme head?"

The entire Assembly then responded: "So be it. Amen."

This august ceremony, adds the historian Janssen, through the representative of the Church, consecrated the reciprocal duties of the sovereign and the people; a contract was affirmed between the nation and the sovereign. Immediately afterwards the coronation and consecration took place. The Church sanctified the temporal order in the person of the King, permeating it with the spirit of Christianity.

Thus, all faithfully respected cultural life was sanctified by supernatural life, and thus life in all its manifestations was profoundly Christian. Life was prayer, and, just as in every being in prayer, life was rich in all possible manifestations of life (wisdom, art) and, at the same time, profoundly humble, forgetful of itself and longing only for the One from whom all good comes.

That admirable balance is broken when the temporal power ceases to serve and seeks only to command. All imbalance is produced by the sin of the evil spirit—*non serviam*. Pride is the beginning of all evil.

This happened in a typical way at the end of the Middle Ages, when Philip the Fair turned the authority consecrated by the Church against her. By the sacrilegious hand of Wilhelm von Nogaret, Philip the Fair seized the Pope, kept him prisoner, and outraged him at Anagní. Seated on his throne with the tiara on his head, holding the keys and the cross in his hands, the old pontiff in whom the Middle Ages had taken refuge was despised by the absolutism of the monarchs that opened the Modern Age.

This rebellion inaugurates in the social realm the gestation of a new spirit that is strengthened as the priesthood is weakened in its prestige (with the Renaissance Popes) and that remains as officially formulated and assured in Luther's rebellion.

Backed by princes and in a certain way heralded by the Renaissance, Luther concentrates his blows on the Roman pontiff, the authentic depositary of grace.

Thus an "absolutist" culture was inaugurated, in which princes did not recognize any rights other than their own wills; the culture was also "naturalistic," because man seeks the expansion of nature. Likewise, it was "rationalist" because man, with his own measures, is sought in all the manifestations of art. Lastly, it was "classicist," because what is sought is a perfection of balance and rationalist order.

A specific case of this culture can be found in the century of Louis XIV in France, where the absolutism of the monarch gained an expansion parallel to the naturalism of Buffon and Fontenelle, the moralism of Bruyére and La Fontaine, the rationalism of Descartes, the humanism of Moliere, the classicism of Corneille and Racine, and the Gallicanism of Bossuet.

At the same time that the anthropocentric world was being lived, it was walking to its dissolution and giving way to the "animal" world, that is, to a world in which man will not adjust his life to human requirements but to subhuman ones, to the animal ones that ask for satisfaction. Thus, for example, Descartes' action ends in Kant's suicide of reason.

Why all of this? The reason is simple: without supernatural grace man cannot achieve the perfection of his nature and of his reason, as the Church teaches in the Vatican Council.[3]

Thus rationalism is inevitably nothing more than a path to the torture of reason; absolutism to the execution of the

3 Vatican I, "Dei Filius" (April 24, 1870), regarding the Catholic faith.

monarchs; naturalism a path to the torture of nature; humanism a path to the torment of the human.

It is likewise inevitable that rationalism ends with the suicide of reason in Kant-Nietzche, absolutism on the scaffold with Louis XVI, naturalism with nineteenth-century materialism, humanism with the animal life of the positivist, classicism with the debauchery of the fantasy of romanticism.

In other words, the first revolution wrought by modern man in supplanting the supernatural will end in the second revolution, which will, in turn, supplant the political to inaugurate the primacy of the economic.

Luther's Revolution inevitably falls into the French Revolution.

The French Revolution is, in substance, the supplanting of the nobility by the bourgeoisie, of politics by economics, of the human by the subhuman, of the rational by the stupid, of the classical by the romantic, of absolutism by democracy.

This is all simply because of the intrinsic logic of revolutions. A revolution in the metaphysical meaning is a rebellion of the inferior against the superior to make the inferior prevail.

With the French Revolution a bourgeois, animal, stupid, and positivist world begins: "animal," because once the *homo naturalis* has been exhausted, the *homo animalis* cannot function. Hence materialism, "stupid and positivist" because, having exhausted reason, that is, the faculty that interprets and unifies facts, that reasons about facts, man has no choice but to limit himself to verifying and seeing the facts and collecting them, that is, positivism.

I have said that this second revolution opens "the era of the economy." Indeed, the nineteenth century is essentially an economist century, as evidenced by the colossal industrial, commercial, and financial expansion that took place in it.

The fact that the century is economist requires that political force be weakened and that it bend to economic demands, just as in the previous era the primacy of the political meant the cultural cancelation of the priesthood. In effect, politics loses its effectiveness because of the democratic understanding of sovereignty promulgated by Rousseau.

It would be wrong to imagine that in an economistic culture the economic task obtains its proper object. On the contrary, for the same reason that the economic act was previously subordinated in its essence to the political and religious, now its economic function must necessarily be inverted.

Indeed so it is, as we have shown in the chapters of this book. An economist economy is inevitably inverted; in it, consumption is in order to produce more, production is in order to sell more, selling is in order to profit more, when the right economic organization demands that finance and commerce be at the service of production and production at the service of consumption and consumption at the service of man and man at the service of God.

An economy thus inverted is inevitably fatal and must end in a tremendous economic catastrophe, in which we seem to find ourselves.

It seems that the moment we currently find ourselves in is the end of the bourgeois economist era.

We are at the end of an age in which the cultural influence of the priesthood is exhausted and practical atheism reigns; the cultural influence of politics is exhausted and demagoguery prevails; the cultural influence of the bourgeois economy, which is going to hand over primacy to the proletariat, is exhausted, and we find ourselves in universal bankruptcy.

We are at the end of the second revolution and the beginning of the third, which is the Communist revolution, the proletarian revolution, in which the worker, placed in the lowest social condition, wants to supplant the bourgeois, the politician, and the priest. He wants to supplant the bourgeois and repudiates the bourgeois economy; he wants to supplant the politician and repudiates governments of authority; he wants to supplant the priesthood and establishes atheism as a system.

Communism imposed in Russia and with a mad desire to spread to all areas of the earth, marks the last of the possible revolutions in a cultural cycle. After it, nothing but chaos is possible.

Let us specify the character of Communism in more detail. The communist is a man who has had his supernatural formality, his natural formality, and his animal formality removed.

What remains of a man from whom those three formalities have been removed? A thing remains, something that walks towards nothingness. What Communism is in reality is the deification of the reality that tends to nothingness. What is the reality that tends to nothing? What is it that is something and yet is nothing by virtue of its formless character? Prime matter. Indeed, Aristotle defines prime matter saying: *Dico autem materiam quae secundum se, nec quid nec quantitas, nec aliud aliquid eorum decitur quibus est ens determinatum* [Now I mean matter, which in itself, is neither whatness nor quantity, nor any other thing determined by those things by which a being is determined].[d]

Prime matter can be everything, from earth to man; but of its own it is none of these things, nothing determined; it is a pure capacity to receive.

Now, in Thomistic language, communism could be defined as that system of life and culture that tends to resolve man into prime matter, something purely formless, chaotic.

Hence, in all manifestations of life, both in social institutions such as family, property, corporation, country, as well as in artistic activities, as well as in science itself,

d It is unclear where the citation is from.

communism is purely formless and chaotic. To confirm it, I refer the reader to those who explain of the Communist reality.

The definition of Communism exposed here coincides with that formulated by the Holy Father in his encyclical letter, although it is taken from another point of view. Indeed, the Holy Father defines Communism by the attitude that it adopts towards the problem of God, which is the main problem that is posed to every man who comes into this world. That attitude can only be one of insolent repudiation, because what rushes into the chaos of prime matter can hate nothing more than the Subsistent Reality.

That attitude of repudiation is as logical as was the attitude of adoration adopted by medieval man informed by supernatural grace; as could be neutrality and secularism, affirmed by the bourgeois of the nineteenth century. What more is there for an animal, a stupid person, deprived of reason and grace, than to dispense with God, whom his imbecility prevents him from knowing?

Hence, only in a culture placed under the rule of the proletariat, as is the Communist culture, is it possible to find an "organized and militant atheism," committed to a "campaign of atheism," as Pope Pius XI said.[e]

Today's Communism is therefore a very deep cultural regression—it is the critical moment of regression immediately prior to death.

What cultural forces are found on the present human scene?

According to the previous considerations, we see that, in what it has of its own, it is almost the final moment in the regressive process that has shaken the world from the Reformation until now.

The milestones of this process can be indicated:

- Renaissance
- Protestant Reformation

e Again, the reference is unclear.

- Cartesian rationalism
- Rousseauian liberalism
- Bourgeois capitalism
- Socialism
- Communism

They are different stages of one same process of degradation, which can find a symbol in the process of corruption that takes place in the human body. Human cultures are like the human body. As long as the body is informed by the immortal soul, the body lives. However, the moment the immortal soul leaves the body, the body becomes lifeless and walks with sure steps until its total dissolution. At the moment of death, the body retains the appearances of a living body: it seems to sleep. The tissues retain their integrity, but little by little they dissolve; corruption nests in its entrails, the cadaverous stench announces this process of corruption, and in the end, nothing will remain of that body but a heap of dust.

The Church was this immortal, self-subsistent soul that gave life to culture.

In the Renaissance and in the Protestant Reformation, the divorce of the Church with culture took place. Culture was left without its life principle, although by virtue of the vital impulse of this principle, it retained all appearances of life. The classical Age, which has had such extraordinary manifestations of culture, can be compared to "in vitro" cultures, which still live after the death of the individual. They live driven by the vitality that has abandoned them; they actually walk to their death.

This is why the entire modern world is a cadaverous world, with the particularity that now, when it is about to dissolve into dust, the types of the various states of decomposition through which it has passed are preserved. Indeed, the Protestant sects remain; Cartesian rationalism perseveres;

Rousseau's liberalism, Voltaireanism continues; bourgeois capitalism lasts alongside socialism and Communism, which embody the characteristic stages corresponding to the process of decomposition at the present moment.

The curious thing is that these delayed stages are locked in a fight with socialism and communism as if they were enemies. In reality, they are brothers at different ages: all the children of the same rebellion marching into the same chaos, although with different steps.

They are all forces of disorder, revolutionary forces in the true sense of the word, because they have rebelled against the One who is First and Foremost and who upholds the normal order of culture.

In this way, all the forces that can be staggered by degrees from Protestantism to communism, form, perhaps without knowing it and without wanting it, a united front of revolution that marches towards chaos.

Opposite these revolutionary forces, which all gravitate towards Moscow, is the Catholic Church.

By its essence, the Church is above the cultural sphere. Her mission is divine: she wants to unite men in Christ, to unite them with God. Her mission is eternal: she, beyond time and space, unites men with divine bonds.

However, and by virtue of its supra-cultural essence, the Church has a great life-giving power for human cultures. The temporal in contact with the eternal is vivified like the earth in contact with the sun, and, on the contrary, removed from its influence, it dies. Hence, from the material elements that could survive from the Greco-Roman world and the barbarian races, the Church has forged the greatest culture that has left its mark on earth: the culture formed by the Church. The Church infused its spirit into the Greco-Roman elements set aside by the Romans and into the Germanic elements brought over by the barbarians. The wonderful thing about medieval culture is the spirit of the Church that breathes in it. It is the spirit of God. It is the Eternal Spirit. We could say that the hierarchy that we discovered in the Middle Ages is nothing more than a condition for the life of the Spirit: let us remember the abundant outpouring of the Spirit in mystical writers (Saint Bernard, Hugh of Saint Victor, Saint Bonaventure), in the architects of the Gothic cathedrals, in the frescoes of Giotto and Fra Angelico, and in the divine prudence of holy kings.

The value of the Middle Ages lies in this admirable outpouring of the Spirit, and not, as historians imagine, in feudal institutions and in the Holy Roman Empire. Feudalism has been a particular realization (one of the possible ones) formed by the supra-cultural influence of the Church. Many other Christian cultures healthier than feudalism are possible.

The Church, by virtue of its essence, which is to sanctify the human and incorporate it into Christ, is driven by an essentially hierarchical movement; she wants order in human accomplishments; she wants the realization of true culture.

This is why her movement is diametrically opposed to the one that shakes the modern world.

Just as the modern world is driven by an impetus of rebellion, of breaking down hierarchies and throwing itself into chaos, so the Church is moved by the Spirit of subordination, of respect for essential hierarchies, of integration into order.

The Church gravitates to Unity; the modern world, to chaos, which is lack of unity.

The Church throws herself into God who unites; the modern world, in the Spirit, of the evil that confuses.

The real opposition between the Church and the modern world arises in the fundamental problem of every man: the problem of God. Just as the Church wants to be united to God with all the forces of her soul, so the modern world wants, with the same impetus of its forces, to be separated from Him and erase His name from the face of the earth.

This is why the Catholic Church is the most typical force among those who oppose the revolutionary forces.

She embodies the movement of re-ascension, just as communism embodies the movement of regression.

This re-ascension is not towards the medieval institutions, those that have passed never to return, like everything that changes, but of re-ascension towards that Eternal Spirit that animated the Middle Ages and that for the same reason is eternal and not of the past nor of the future.

The Church wants the return of culture to God, who is *Primum Principium*. She wants to establish order by the primacy of the first hierarchy, the priesthood.

However, it is fair to remember that the visible members of the Church are not in a position at the moment to fully carry out this movement of re-ascension.

Although the Church herself, as the bride of Christ, is "without spot or wrinkle or any such thing... holy and without blemish,"[f] nevertheless, in the life of Christians, she is in a deplorable state of decay. Catholics have been contaminated with the venom of five centuries of apostasy. Catholics have made an alliance with the Renaissance, with classical naturalism, with the Protestant spirit of free examination, with liberalism, with the repugnant bourgeoisie, and more. Catholics have become worldly and the Immaculate Spouse of Christ is imprisoned and suffocated under the thick crust of modern poisons.

In order to recover her cultural primacy, the Church needs to undergo a profound purification in the hearts of Christians, a purification that will consume these poisons and leave free passage to the outpourings of the Spirit.

This purification is taking place in the Catholic Action movement, which is and should be a movement of sanctification in Christ. His Holiness Pius XI acknowledges

---

f Eph 5:27.

this action of the Holy Spirit when in *Caritate Christi Compulsi* he writes:

> For most certainly a very powerful afflatus [a divine impulse or inspiration] of the Holy Spirit is rushing through all lands, and is moving the hearts, especially the hearts of the young, to mount upwards to the highest summits of the Christian law, and, raising them above the vain observance of men, makes them ready to undertake even the most arduous deeds. This divine afflatus, We say, stirs the souls of all, even those who were unwilling, filling them with an intimate solicitude, and gives the yearning for God even to those who do not dare to acknowledge it.[g]

g Pius XI, "Caritate Christi Compulsi," 10.

Appendix A

Bull *Detestabilis* by Sixtus V

Sixtus Bishop, Servant of the Servants of God, for perpetual remembrance.

The detestable voracity of greed and the insatiable greed for profit, the root of all evils, blinds men's minds in such a way that many, greedy for profit, fall miserably into the snares and snares of the devil, because that ancient enemy of the human race cautiously slips into various deceits and fallacies and oppresses men fascinated by the sweetness of profit and drags them to submerge them in the maelstrom of usury, hateful to God and men, condemned by the sacred canons, contrary to Christian charity, and while they seek vain and terrestrial riches they lose the true and heavenly ones, as recently we have heard with great pain that it occurs in some provinces.

Because many, using the honest partnership contract as an excuse for their usury, give their money or other things to merchants, artisans, merchants, or other people with the guarantee of their merchandise, shops, warehouses, bakeries; or deliver in partnership cattle or certain animals to farmers or shepherds or any other person on the condition that the capital, as it is called, of all money, animals, or things always remains safe and intact in favor of the one who contributes to the company not industry or work but rather money, animals, or similar things, so that all the risk and damage falls on the other partner and thus they agree in various ways against the equity and justice of the partnership contract; and to the partners themselves with whom they make the contract, generally poor and needy partners who live from their work and industry, force them to return the capital regardless of their fate and at the same time determine and prescribe what the partner must to pay them, per month or per year, while the company lasts, a certain profit, a certain percentage; and they want this sum and amount to be fixed and determined without paying attention to the fact that this benefit is deducted from the entries and exits that are kept in the books, nor that the benefit or loss is variable; they want it fixed and determined, disinterested in work and the care of carrying out the calculations of society.

Therefore, We who judge as the main and proper function of our pastoral solicitude to direct in the way of health, with the help of divine grace, the flock of the Lord entrusted to Us safe from all danger and risk of eternal life, wanting to remove, as soon as with the help of God we can, the contagion of this evil before it spreads further to the common ruin of the faithful, using the fullness of our apostolic power by the present constitution that is to be valid forever, we condemn and reprove all contracts, conventions, and pacts that have to be made in which guarantees are given to the people who deliver money, animals, or any other things in society that even if they suffer bankruptcy, damage, or loss, the capital must always be returned except and in full by the partner who receives it, or that he has to respond with a certain sum or quantity every month or year while the company lasts.

We establish that these contracts, conventions, and pacts must be considered as usurious and therefore must be considered illegal; and that henceforth it is not lawful for those who invest their money, animals, or other things in society, to agree and agree with respect to a certain profit; nor oblige with an agreement or promise, they have agreed with respect to certain or indeterminate profit, to the borrowing partners to return the capital safe and full when it has fortuitously perished or disappeared.

And we categorically prohibit the creation of companies with these pacts and conditions that involve the vice of usury from now on.

Appendix B

Bull *Vix Pervenit* by Benedict XIV

On Usury and Other Dishonest Profits

To the Venerable Brothers, Patriarchs, Archbishops, Bishops and Ordinary Clergy of Italy.

Venerable Brothers, Greetings and Apostolic Benediction.

Hardly had the new controversy (namely, whether certain contracts should be held valid) come to our attention, when several opinions began spreading in Italy that hardly seemed to agree with sound doctrine; We decided that We must remedy this. If We did not do so immediately, such an evil might acquire new force by delay and silence. If we neglected our duty, it might even spread further, shaking those cities of Italy so far not affected.

Therefore We decided to consult with a number of the Cardinals of the Holy Roman Church, who are renowned for their knowledge and competence in theology and canon law. We also called upon many from the regular clergy who were outstanding in both the faculty of theology and that of canon law. We chose some monks, some mendicants, and finally some from the regular clergy. As presiding officer, We appointed one with degrees in both canon and civil law, who had lengthy court experience. We chose the past July 4 for the meeting at which We explained the nature of the whole business. We learned that all had known and considered it already.

2. We then ordered them to consider carefully all aspects of the matter, meanwhile searching for a solution; after this consideration, they were to write out their conclusions. We did not ask them to pass judgment on the contract which gave rise to the controversy since the many documents they would need were not available. Rather We asked that they establish a fixed teaching on usury, since the opinions recently spread abroad seemed to contradict the Church's doctrine. All complied with these orders. They gave their opinions publicly in two convocations, the first of which was held in our presence last July 18, the other last August 1; then they submitted their opinions in writing to the secretary of the convocation.

3. Indeed they proved to be of one mind in their opinions.

I. The nature of the sin called usury has its proper place and origin in a loan contract. This financial contract between consenting parties demands, by its very nature, that one return to another only as much as he has received. The sin rests on the fact that sometimes the creditor desires more than he has given. Therefore he contends some gain is owed him beyond that which he loaned, but any gain which exceeds the amount he gave is illicit and usurious.

II. One cannot condone the sin of usury by arguing that the gain is not great or excessive, but rather moderate or small; neither can it be condoned by arguing that the borrower is rich; nor even by arguing that the money borrowed is not left idle, but is spent usefully, either to increase one's fortune, to purchase new estates, or to engage in business transactions. The law governing loans consists necessarily in the equality of what is given and returned; once the equality has been established, whoever demands more than that violates the terms of the loan. Therefore if one receives interest, he must make restitution according to the commutative bond of justice; its function in human contracts is to assure equality for each one. This law is to be observed in a holy manner. If not observed exactly, reparation must be made.

III. By these remarks, however, We do not deny that at times together with the loan contract certain other titles-which are not at all intrinsic to the contract-may run parallel with it. From these other titles, entirely just and legitimate reasons arise to demand something over and above the amount due on the contract. Nor is it denied that it is very often possible for someone, by means of contracts differing entirely from loans, to spend and invest money legitimately either to provide oneself with an annual income or to engage in legitimate trade and business. From these types of contracts honest gain may be made.

IV. There are many different contracts of this kind. In these contracts, if equality is not maintained, whatever is received over and above what is fair is a real injustice. Even though it may not fall under the precise rubric of usury (since all reciprocity, both open and hidden, is absent), restitution is obligated. Thus if everything is done correctly and weighed in the scales of justice, these same legitimate contracts suffice to provide a standard and a principle for engaging in commerce and fruitful business for the common good. Christian minds should not think that gainful commerce can flourish by usuries or other similar injustices. On the contrary We learn from divine Revelation that justice raises up nations; sin, however, makes nations miserable.

V. But you must diligently consider this, that some will falsely and rashly persuade themselves-and such people can be found anywhere-that together with loan contracts there are other legitimate titles or, excepting loan contracts, they might convince themselves that other just contracts exist, for which it is permissible to receive a moderate amount of interest. Should any one think like this, he will oppose not only the judgment of the Catholic Church on usury, but also common human sense and natural reason. Everyone knows that man is obliged in many instances to help his fellows with a simple, plain loan. Christ Himself teaches this: "Do not refuse to lend to him who asks you." In many circumstances, no other true and just contract may be possible except for a loan. Whoever therefore wishes to follow his conscience must first diligently inquire if, along with the loan, another category exists by means of which the gain he seeks may be lawfully attained.

4. This is how the Cardinals and theologians and the men most conversant with the canons, whose advice We had asked for in this most serious business, explained their opinions. Also We devoted our private study to this matter before the congregations were convened, while they were in session, and again after they had been held; for We read the opinions of these outstanding men most diligently. Because of this, We approve and confirm whatever is contained in the opinions above, since the professors of Canon Law and Theology, scriptural evidence, the decrees of previous popes, and the authority of Church councils and the Fathers all seem to enjoin it. Besides, We certainly know the authors who hold the opposite opinions and also those who either support and defend those authors or at least who seem to give them consideration. We are also aware that the theologians of regions neighboring those in which the controversy had its origin undertook the defense of the truth with wisdom and seriousness.

5. Therefore We address these encyclical letters to all Italian Archbishops, Bishops, and priests to make all of you aware of these matters. Whenever Synods are held or sermons preached or instructions on sacred doctrine given, the above opinions must be adhered to strictly. Take great care that no one in your dioceses dares to write or preach the contrary;

however if any one should refuse to obey, he should be subjected to the penalties imposed by the sacred canons on those who violate Apostolic mandates.

6. Concerning the specific contract which caused these new controversies, We decide nothing for the present; We also shall not decide now about the other contracts in which the theologians and canonists lack agreement. Rekindle your zeal for piety and your conscientiousness so that you may execute what We have given.

7. First of all, show your people with persuasive words that the sin and vice of usury is most emphatically condemned in the Sacred Scriptures; that it assumes various forms and appearances in order that the faithful, restored to liberty and grace by the blood of Christ, may again be driven headlong into ruin. Therefore, if they desire to invest their money, let them exercise diligent care lest they be snatched by cupidity, the source of all evil; to this end, let them be guided by those who excel in doctrine and the glory of virtue.

8. In the second place, some trust in their own strength and knowledge to such an extent that they do not hesitate to give answers to those questions which demand considerable knowledge of sacred theology and of the canons. But it is essential for these people, also, to avoid extremes, which are always evil. For instance, there are some who judge these matters with such severity that they hold any profit derived from money to be illegal and usurious; in contrast to them, there are some so indulgent and so remiss that they hold any gain whatsoever to be free of usury. Let them not adhere too much to their private opinions. Before they give their answer, let them consult a number of eminent writers; then let them accept those views which they understand to be confirmed by knowledge and authority. And if a dispute should arise, when some contract is discussed, let no insults be hurled at those who hold the contrary opinion; nor let it be asserted that it must be severely censured, particularly if it does not lack the

support of reason and of men of reputation. Indeed clamorous outcries and accusations break the chain of Christian love and give offense and scandal to the people.

9. In the third place, those who desire to keep themselves free and untouched by the contamination of usury and to give their money to another in such a manner that they may receive only legitimate gain should be admonished to make a contract beforehand. In the contract they should explain the conditions and what gain they expect from their money. This will not only greatly help to avoid concern and anxiety, but will also confirm the contract in the realm of public business. This approach also closes the door on controversies-which have arisen more than once-since it clarifies whether the money, which has been loaned without apparent interest, may actually contain concealed usury.

10. In the fourth place We exhort you not to listen to those who say that today the issue of usury is present in name only, since gain is almost always obtained from money given to another. How false is this opinion and how far removed from the truth! We can easily understand this if we consider that the nature of one contract differs from the nature of another. By the same token, the things which result from these contracts will differ in accordance with the varying nature of the contracts. Truly an obvious difference exists between gain which arises from money legally, and therefore can be upheld in the courts of both civil and canon law, and gain which is illicitly obtained, and must therefore be returned according to the judgments of both courts. Thus, it is clearly invalid to suggest, on the grounds that some gain is usually received from money lent out, that the issue of usury is irrelevant in our times.

11. These are the chief things We wanted to say to you. We hope that you may command your faithful to observe what these letters prescribe; and that you may undertake effective remedies if disturbances should be stirred up among your

people because of this new controversy over usury or if the simplicity and purity of doctrine should become corrupted in Italy. Finally, to you and to the flock committed to your care, We impart the Apostolic Benediction.

Given in Rome at St. Mary Major, November 1, 1745, the sixth year of Our Pontificate.

Appendix C

Regarding Loans at Interest

In order to fully understand the nature of a system in which the loan at interest is abolished, I think it is fitting to reproduce some pages of the book *Du Prét á Interét ou Des Causes Théologiques du Socialisme* by M. l'Abbé Jules Morel, Lecoffre Fils et Cie., Paris, 1873.

On pg. 132 he writes: "Is it necessary to say then, that the use of money, according to the Church's system, should abolish banking, state loans, financial companies, and in general everything that allows the circulation of capital necessary for a trade, both domestic and foreign? If you want to talk about agiotage, the stock market, speculation, everything that turns commerce and trade into a game, everything that accelerates competition to the point of substituting health for fever, yes, certainly the desire and legislation of the Church would be to place an insurmountable veto on it. However, if you want to talk about a regular, thoughtful, and measured trade, compatible with the eternal goods that we must arrive at after having passed through temporal goods, no: the Church, which is useful to all, had understood all the benefits, and has hastened to trace the path.

The first bankers in the world, chronologically speaking, have been Italians, the bankers of Florence, Siena, Pisa, Genoa, and Venice who respected the Christian faith and observed its morality. However, when the demon of profit wanted to make the honest profits of Christians degenerate into the Mammon of iniquity, then the vigilant papacy intervened to suppress all this accursed science of money orders, credits, fictitious mandates and all of these fictions that today replace healthy reality.

Saint Pius V has an admirable bull on the changes (*In eam pronostro*, January 28, 1571) and some of the paragraphs we transcribe here:

> And so, having reached our ears that the legitimate use of exchanges, introduced by public necessity and utility, was frequently depraved by the greed for illicit gain, so that usury was exercised under its pretext, we judged that we should answer the questions that were recently made to us, with this decree that will be valid forever. . . .
>
> First (then) we condemn all those exchanges which are called fictitious, (elsewhere, dry), and are so devised that the contracting parties at certain market places or at other localities pretend to solemnize exchanges; at which places those who receive money, actually hand over their letters of exchange, but they are not sent, or they are so sent that, when the time has passed they are brought back void, whence they had set out; or, even when no letters of this kind were handed over, the money is finally demanded with interest, where the contract had been solemnized; for between givers and receivers even from the

beginning it had been so decided, or surely such was the intention, and there is no one who in the marketplaces or the above mentioned places makes payment, when such letters are received.

And similar to this evil is also that, when money or deposits or by another name fictitious exchanges are handed over so that afterwards in the same place or elsewhere they are paid back with interest.

But even in the exchanges which are called real, sometimes, as it is reported to me, bankers put off the prescribed term of payment, when a profit has been received according to tacit or expressed agreement or even only a promise.

All these things we declare to be usurious, and strictly prohibit their being done.[a]

For this reason, in order to suppress, as far as We can, the occasions of sin that exist in the exchanges and frauds of usurers, We decree that from now on no one dares, be it from the beginning or otherwise, to agree to a certain and determined interest, even in the case of insolvency, and that no real changes can be made except for the first markets, where they are made, and where they are not made for the first installments, following the approved usage of the country, completely banishing the abuse of making changes for markets that will come in a second place or later or for equally remote deadline.

But it will still be necessary to take care that when an exchange is made in the near term, the

a These four paragraphs are taken from Dz 1081-1082.

> remoteness or proximity of the places where the payment is made is taken into account so that there is no reason to practice usury if the payment term is greater than what is required by the geographical position of the cities where the payments must be made.

All this seems too superficial and evasive. Let us take a deeper look. The Pontiff declares that the use of the exchange is legitimate, that this use has been introduced by public necessity, but that illicit gains have been introduced on the occasion of the exchange, and in the course of the bull, he gives the explanation. The exchange is according to its nature when it transports money from one place to another and when it procures the currency of another country where the trade is carried out, for the currency of the country to which the merchant belongs.

Be it for this transport, be it for this change of currency, the exchange is entitled to a legitimate gain. If, however, instead of a real exchange or even with a real exchange, unnecessary, but voluntarily consented, delays in payment of the exchange are introduced, so that the money bears interest during this period of time, usury is placed on the exchange and hence exchange becomes a sin.

It is therefore truly the commercial loan, with its infinite varieties of form, that Saint Pius V condemns here.

Further on[1] Jules Morel studies how a merchant or industrialist, or everyone who is in possession of productive assets, could procure capital without resorting to interest loans, which is essentially bad. He writes:

Rent is legitimate in itself since it is the income of a productive source: the rent for a house, the rent for a field.

1 Jules Morel, *Du Prét á Interét ou Des Causes Théologiques du Socialisme* (Paris: Lecoffre Fils et Cie, 1873), 139. It is unclear where the quote ends.

Therefore, if this rent is sold for a capital that is its fair representation, a fair contract is made. This proves how false it is to say that the Church does not recognize any value in the use of money since it condemns usury. Not at all. The Church perfectly admits that an owner abandons the right that he has to the income from his field for an indefinite period of time. Yet the sale of this rent is not the same as the sale of the field. Indeed, if the field were sold, the money from the sale would pass from the hands of the seller who would lose not only the rent but also the funds that this field produced; while in the contract in question, only the rent changes ownership while the funds remain in the hands of the owner.

The sale of the rent is simply a loan on a property that produces interest. But what can be done so that this lucrative loan for the lender and onerous for the borrower is not usurious? Here the insight of St. Pius V shines, along with his desire to meet all needs.

Where does the injustice of the usurer come from? It comes from the fact that he can fix the time in which the money will be repaid with all the fruits produced during the interval. Here, on the contrary, the capitalist will abandon his consistent capital in the rent to the person who wants to make use of it without being able to say: the term has expired, pay!

This provision favorable to the borrower and begins to restore the balance between the borrower and the lender. However, there is still more. What assures that the one borrowing not be fascinated by the brightness and comfort of capital, when he has exchanged the rent of his field for the possession of this seductive capital? It is that he had in hand this income from which he has the pain of parting, while he who goes to the usurer does not part with anything and takes everything that fascinates him and, on the other hand, this mortgaged income on the field is going to be enough for the payment of interest on the capital lent: which gives the borrower all his security and freedom of action, as long as he is the holder of the capital.

It is thus loss, but moderate loss on the one hand, which prevents fascination and abuse, and on the other, tranquility regarding the time in which interest must be paid, which keeps man in possession of his freedom: such are the essential conditions of constituted income; they restore the balance between the borrower and the lender.

What a request of the Church for the weak! Yet, this is still not all. If the funds that maintain the perpetual income perish due to any cause, will the borrower be encumbered with the income that must be paid when he does not have the instrument that produced it? No. From this moment on he has no further obligation.

There's more. He who has lent the capital cannot retake it, unless for one reason or another the rent is not paid. However, he who has made the loan will never be able to free his house or field from the mortgage that weighs on them? He can. Hence the bull of Saint Pius V requires that the income constituted be redeemable by the borrower at the time he wants the loaned capital repaid.

Thus the rights of the borrower, of the relatively weak, are defended by the Church against the omnipotence, fascination, and tyranny of the capitalist.

But why is the income not redeemable by the lender as well as by the borrower? Since in such a contract the balance would be broken. The borrower would be forced to repay in a fixed term or, what is worse, at the will of the lender, which would only have an oppressive, fictitious, unproductive use of the loaned capital and he would ultimately be a victim of the contract that he would have made to remedy his momentary plight or at least that seemed so.

Such are the conditions of the rent, decreed by the famous bull of Saint Pius V *Cum onus apostolicos servitutis* of 1569.

It is now seen that these conditions curb the desire to contract a loan and the desire to lend, a double desire, which if not restrained ruins the present and the future. Do you want to get a loan? Yes, but you will not be able to contract on inconsistent and impalpable values such as your credit, your merit, the beautiful operations that you will carry out in the future, the magic of credit, the game, in a word, in which you promise to win. You cannot contract a loan except on a possession that you already have, which is the fruit of your sweat or that of your elders, and within the limits of this possession. You limit it and you affect it to the payment of the capital that you will receive with interest.

Do you want to lend? However, you will not be able to do it without getting rid of your capital for an indefinite period of time that you will not be able to claim. Do you want to lend? Yes, but you will not be able to do it without losing the right to rent, in the event that the mortgaged fund perishes due to *force majeure*.

What would be the situation of the States, if they had followed these rules of Saint Pius V? Perhaps in public crises, to which families as well are subject to private crises, could they not contract a loan to lighten the tax? But of course. States have properties, forests, castles, mines, and the like that they can mortgage and receive an income on these properties and they could thus contract the loan. They will be settled later when better days come. However, will they be able to contract loans without reason or measure, following the fantasy of their spirit of conquest or disorderly ambition? Will they be able to crush future generations, devour them at a discount, ruin them in advance, unload on them like prodigal parents on their children? By no means. No healthy credit will be found in the past, that is, on savings, on what was earned, what was acquired in previous times. No credit will be made on a world that does not yet exist and will be deprived of the means by which it could be released when it sees the light of day.

The Church has foreseen all this. The body of this prudent mother has been passed over as just as her commandments have passed over: confidence has been placed in a new political economy, forged in the heads of philosophers. The world has allowed itself to be fascinated by the magic of credit in a century in which the word "magic" causes laughter, as if it were something exclusive to idiots and since everyone is hooked by this magic, everyone wants to lend and the State only seeks loans, it would not be surprising if France raised her debt to fifty thousand and all her loans were covered. They have rightly mocked Louis XV, the most miserable of the kings of the old regime, and behold, democracy imitates his excesses, saying like him: After me the deluge!

This book by Jules Morel, published in 1873, is literally a prophecy of what was to happen in our century with the loan at interest. Here is the translation of chapter 14, entitled: "The abolition of interest would bring us back to the golden age."

Now let's discuss the relationship between the scourges of the stock market and the doctrine of the Church on the loan at interest.

First of all, the securities that are traded on the stock market carry, in their entirety, interest. Due to this, the abandonment of the interest would constitute by itself a serious impediment to the operations of the stock market. However, there would still be the negotiation of the shares that represent an industry in exploitation. Couldn't the rise and fall be applied to those values, even if they were deprived of the interest stipulation that they now carry?

In this regard, we will note that interest, like the rise and fall of shares, is also based on a singular foundation: the anticipated value of the benefits that could be obtained, either with the money that I lend you and while you retain it, either, with my part of ownership in such a factory that is or will be in operation, but which has not yet given performance because a first fiscal year has not been completed or a new fiscal year has not yet begun. Since a value is not put into circulation if it is not trusting in the rise; and the fall is nothing more than the first bankruptcy of that hope. Every value released is released upwards, from which it results that all interest and all stock market negotiations are based on the *lucrum cessans* applied to a probability, to a possibility of gain that someone deprives himself of to pass it on to another. Since this gain may exist, but does not yet exist, it is rightly called, not purchase, but speculation; and in the measure that speculation overlaps speculation, skyrocketing, that gain, increasingly random, becomes *agio*, a wild stock market game, all or nothing, to end in millions or suicide.

That inverted pyramid rests, then, as on its tip, on the sale of *lucrum cessans.* On that foundation it oscillates, seeking a balance that cannot be preserved. But, once again, what is this *lucrum cessans* that has produced such extraordinary and unexpected effects for its very inventors? It is neither more nor less than this external title that the genius—really incomprehensible—of Saint Thomas Aquinas, of the doctor more angelic than human, did not admit at any price; because the *lucrum cessans* sold what it did not yet have, and what it could, for many reasons, not have, being precisely those anxieties the motives for the rise and fall: *Recompensationem vero damni quod consideratur in hoc quod de Pecunia sua non lucratur, non potest in pactum deducere, quia non debet vendare id quod non dum habet et potest impedari multipliciter ab habendo* [But the compensation for the loss which is considered in the fact that he does not gain from his money, cannot be brought into an agreement, because he must not sell what he does not have while he has it and can be prevented in many ways from having it.].[b]

Therefore, if it is prohibited, as it is indeed, to exploit the *lucrum cessans,* to sell what is not yet possessed, what may never be possessed, there is no more interest, nor speculation, nor fierce competition, nor stock market; business is all done

b The reference is unclear.

with constant money. With the pandemonium devastated, the demons flee. In three prophetic lines, Saint Thomas denounces the injustice on which the entire economy of the nineteenth century rests, and the revolutions that come from it as a necessary consequence.

Lord Jesus, what a man you had given to your Church in that beautiful thirteenth century, the last of the temporal splendor of your Spouse! How good is the *Summa* of that doctor next to your Gospels, in the bosom of the councils!

Let's get back to earthly things. The worker is exploited by the employer, even though he is human, even though he sometimes feels like a brother and a father towards his worker. However, the employer is prevented from being effectively paternal, or fraternal, or humanitarian, because he, in turn, suffers the exploitation of the rabid competition created by the loan at interest, and agitated by the stock market to the point of delirium. The employer cannot be good to the worker: his profits are disputed by a crowd of visible and invisible enemies, and he has lost his religion. He has abandoned religion, because he has even less time than the worker. If the latter's arms work almost seven days a week, a chaos of worries and uncertainties obsesses the former's head, during the same time. The appeasement of society, the necessary decline of the commercial whirlwind, therefore depends on the reestablishment of the law of Sunday rest and the law against usury. Anything you want to do outside of that will be worth as much as opposing a few blades of straw to the fall of a great building.

Every man who works, or who forces another to work on Sunday, deserves to be stoned, as in the people of God; and every man who lends at interest, would merit the same punishment. There are two commandments, and both form one: love of God and love of neighbor. The highest expression of the first is the sanctification of Sunday, and the highest expression of the second is the renunciation of usury.

We already know for sure that the objections will rain down, and we are prepared.

It would be very desirable if all trade were done in cash, but that is simply impossible. The colossal enterprises of finance and industry, of which this century boasts, could no longer be carried out, since if interest and the stock market were suppressed, there would no longer be a machine that had the power to suck in capital. — That's true: but what harm would there be if colossal companies were replaced by sensible companies?

There would be no way to feed cities of one, two and three million inhabitants. — God willing! Is it necessary for the peoples to have those monstrous heads? What is necessary is that they stop having them. The cities of large-scale industry are always the cities of the greatest lawlessness. Look at your Universal Exposition in Paris, immediately followed by the Commune, and how all the kings who had come to visit our industrial marvels in the crowded palace, so soon returned to visit their deserted palace. It is also worth noting here that the city of Lyon, which was the first to practice usury in France, is today the most socialist city. In short, how will it be done when money can no longer be found at interest? — It will be saved. There will be a rotation fund, which will have its guarantee in a reserve fund. — That's fine, but someone may need a loan, and no one will want to lend without interest, except to a poor person, and as little as possible. — This is true — So? —Then, whoever needs money, and is not poor, will sell an income, small or large, on his property. These assets will pay interest through usufruct, while they exist, like all real assets that are perishable, and only the one who sold the rent will have the right to rescue when he wants and when he can. Saint Pius V, another universal genius, a witness to the growth of commerce, offered that Catholic resource to the transactions of the transatlantic navy that needed them. However, the purchaser of the income may not demand the reimbursement of it in capital, and that is what constitutes the profound difference between what lends at interest on a pledge contract, and what restores commutative justice in this kind of transaction.

You will still have an easier time finding capital, if you are honest and skillful, the only two qualities that deserve it. There is no one who wants to lend to the rich for free, yet everyone will nevertheless want to make their money fruitful. It will be a matter, then, of rightly giving it, and this can be done through the partnership contract. This is a legitimate society, in which the interested parties will take great care, because in it profits and losses are shared: *Cum periculo ipsius mutualis mercator de ea pecunia negotiatestur, vel artifex operator* [With the risk of the mutual trader, the money is traded on it or the specialist works][c] says the admirable Saint Thomas. No one will have the privilege of escaping the conditions of all earthly goods, which are subject by nature to human accidents; and in this way, the profits will be legitimate. You speak a lot about the association of capitals: that is the only true and good association.

However, that association through the loan at interest that wants to make earthly goods secure goods for one of the parties, permanent goods like eternal goods, goods endowed with a necessary growth, which come and go without any anxiety, who go out skinny and return fat, from generation to generation, goods inaccessible to the calamities that other men share: don't you see where you are going with those goods that monopolize everything, that absorb everything, that devour the substance of the human race? They create kings who will not only reign, who will not govern only from the top of that unique domain that the powerful possess over the assets of the subjects, translated into taxes. You will have the new kings of finance, who, becoming the arbiters of your

c Again, the reference is unclear.

private fortune, the true owners of your private properties, will give their hidden domination a frightening amplitude. The world of usury, with the current centralization, will resemble, without thinking about it, that Egypt of Joseph's time, where there was only one owner, Pharaoh, of whom permission needed to be asked in order to eat the bread and move the hand or the foot.

The question of usury is the question of earthly life. After the issue of salvation, there is no other issue greater in the universality of human interests.

Bibliography

Andrew W. Mellon. "Interview." *Evening Standard* (London), November 27, 1928.

Benedict XIV. "Vix Pervenit." Encyclical, Rome, November 1, 1745.

Berdiaeff, Nicolas. *Le christianisme et la Lutte des classes.* Translated by I. P. and H. M. Editions du Dromadaire, 1932.

Berdyaev, Nicholas. *Christianity and Class War.* Translated by Donald Attwater. London: Sheed & Ward, 1934.

Berdyaev, Nikolai. "The New Middle Ages." In *The End of Our Time*, translated by Donald Attwater, 67–120. New York: Sheed & Ward, 1933.

Council of Vienne. "Ex Gravi Ad Nos." Decree.

De Maeztu, Ramiro. *La Prensa*, October 20, 1932.

Fallon, Valére. *Economie Sociale.*

First Lateran Council. *Canons.*

Fisher, Irving. *L'illusion de la monnaie stable.*

Ford, Henry. *Ma vie et mon oeuvre; Aujourd'hui et demain.*

———. *Today and Tomorrow.* Boca Raton, FL: CRC Press, 2003.

Fried, Ferdinand. *La Fin du Capitalisme.*

La Tour du Pin, René. *Vers un ordre social Chretien.*

Leo XIII. "Rerum Novarum." Encyclical, Rome, May 15, 1891.

Lima, Alceu Amoroso. *Esbozo de una Introducción a la Economía Moderna.*

Lucius, Pierre. *Faillite du capitalisme?... Une explication de la crise mondiale*. Impr. J. Dumoulin, 1932.

Malcor, Marcel. "L'économie contemporaine." *Nova et Vetera* 4, no. 1 (January–March 1929): 49–75.

———. "L'économie contemporaine : le crédit ou l''usure'." *Nova et Vetera* 6, no. 3 (July 1931): 265–284.

———. "L'économie contemporaine : travail, assurances, capitalisme." *Nova et Vetera* 6, no. 2 (April–June 1931): 122–158.

Maritain, Jacques. "Religion and Culture." In *Essays in Order*, 1–61. New York: Macmillan, 1931.

———. *Religion et culture*. Paris: Desclée, 1930.

———. *Three Reformers: Luther, Descartes, Rousseau*. London: Sheen & Ward, 1928.

Meinvielle, Julio. *Concepción católica de la economía*. Buenos Aires, Argentina: Cursos de Cultura Católica, 1936.

———. *Concepción católica de la economía*. Electronic ed. Arturo Ruiz Freites IVE, 2017.

Mireaux, Emile. *Les Miracles du Crédit*.

Morel, Jules. *Du Prét á Interét ou Des Causes Théologiques du Socialisme*. Paris: Lecoffre Fils et Cie, 1873.

Noguer, Narciso. *Cuestiones candentes sobre la propiedad y el socialismo*.

Peter, Edward N. *The 1917 Pio-Benedictine Code of Canon Law in English*. San Francisco: Ignatius Press, 2001.

Pius XI. "Caritate Christi Compulsi." Encyclical, Rome, May 3, 1932.

———. "Quadragesimo Anno." Encyclical, Rome, Italy, May 15, 1931.

Taylor, Frederick Winslow. *The Principles of Scientific Management*. New York, Harper & Brothers, 1919.

Taylorism. In *Encyclopaedia Briannica*, by The Editors of Encyclopaedia Britannica.

Thomas Aquinas. *Commentary on Aristotle's Politics*. Translated by Richard J. Regan. Indianapolis: Hackett Publishing, 2007.

Union Internationale d'Etudes Sociales. *Code Social: Esquisse d'une synthese sociale catholique*. Montreal: Éditions de L'École Sociale Populaire, 1944.

Vatican I. "Dei Filius." April 24, 1870.

Vinsel, Lee. *Moving Violations: Automobiles, Experts, and Regulations in the United States*. Baltimore: Johns Hopkins University Press, 2019.

Weiss, Alberto, O.P. *Apologia del Cristianismo*. Vol. 8. Barcelona: Juan Gili, 1906.

Index of Authors

Index of Citations

Made in the USA
Monee, IL
04 November 2026

67384612R00118